The Complete Book of Business Legal Forms

The Complete Book of Business Legal Forms

James C. Ray

Attorney at Law

SPHINX® PUBLISHING

AN IMPRINT OF SOURCEBOOKS, INC.®
NAPERVILLE, ILLINOIS
www.SphinxLegal.com

First Edition: 2008

Published by: **Sphinx® Publishing, An Imprint of Sourcebooks, Inc.®**

<u>Naperville Office</u>
P.O. Box 4410
Naperville, Illinois 60567-4410
630-961-3900
Fax: 630-961-2168
www.SphinxLegal.com
www.sourcebooks.com

This publication is designed to provide accurate and authoritative information in regard to the subject matter covered. It is sold with the understanding that the publisher is not engaged in rendering legal, accounting, or other professional service. If legal advice or other expert assistance is required, the services of a competent professional person should be sought.
From a Declaration of Principles Jointly Adopted by a Committee of the American Bar Association and a Committee of Publishers and Associations

This product is not a substitute for legal advice.

Disclaimer required by Texas statutes.

Library of Congress Cataloging-in-Publication Data

Ray, James C.
  The Complete Book of Business Legal Forms / by James C. Ray.
     p. cm.
  Includes index.
  ISBN 978-1-57248-663-8 (pbk. : alk. paper) 1. Contracts--United States--Forms. I. Title.
  KF801.A65R39 2008
  346.73020269--dc22
                              2008012738

Printed and bound in the United States of America.

SB — 10 9 8 7 6 5 4 3 2

Contents

How to Use the CD-ROM

Thank you for purchasing *The Complete Book of Business Legal Forms*. In this book, we have worked hard to compile exactly what you need to run your business. To make this material even more useful, we have included every document in the book on the CD-ROM that is attached to the inside back cover of the book.

You can use these forms just as you would use the forms in the book. Print them out, fill them in, and use them however you need. You can also fill in the forms directly on your computer. Just identify the form you need, open it, click on the space where the information should go, and input your information. Customize each form for your particular needs. Use them over and over again.

The CD-ROM is compatible with both PC and Mac operating systems. (While it should work with either operating system, we cannot guarantee that it will work with your particular system and we cannot provide technical assistance.) To use the forms on your computer, you will need to use Adobe Reader. The CD-ROM does not contain this program. You can download this program from Adobe's website at **www.adobe.com**. Click on the "Get Adobe Reader" icon to begin the download process and follow the instructions.

Once you have Adobe Reader installed, insert the CD-ROM into your computer. Double-click on the icon representing the disc on your desktop or go through your hard drive to identify the drive that contains the disc and click on it.

Once opened, you will see the files contained on the CD-ROM listed as "Form #: [Form Title]." Open the file you need through Adobe Reader. You may print the form to fill it out manually at this point, or your can use the "Hand Tool" and click on the appropriate line to fill it in using your computer.

Any time you see bracketed information, "[ ]," on the form, you can click on it and delete the bracketed information from your final form. This information is only a reference guide to assist you in filling in the forms and should be removed from your final version. Once all your information is filled in, you can print your filled-in form.

NOTE: *Adobe Reader does not allow you to save the PDF with the boxes filled in.*

• • • • •

Purchasers of this book are granted a license to use the forms contained in it for their own personal use. By purchasing this book, you have also purchased a limited license to use all forms on the accompanying CD-ROM. The license limits you to personal use only and all other copyright laws must be adhered to. No claim of copyright is made in any government form reproduced in the book or on the CD-ROM. You are free to modify the forms and tailor them to your specific situation.

The author and publisher have attempted to provide the most current and up-to-date information available. However, the courts, Congress, and your state's legislatures review, modify, and change laws on an ongoing basis, as well as create new laws from time to time. By the very nature of the information and due to the continual changes in our legal system, to be sure that you have the current and best information for your situation, you should consult a local attorney or research the current laws yourself.

• • • • •

This publication is designed to provide accurate and authoritative information in regard to the subject matter covered. It is sold with the understanding that the publisher is not engaged in rendering legal, accounting, or other professional service. If legal advice or other expert assistance is required, the services of a competent professional person should be sought.

> —*From a Declaration of Principles Jointly Adopted by a Committee of the American Bar Association and a Committee of Publishers and Associations*

This product is not a substitute for legal advice.

> —*Disclaimer required by Texas statutes*

Using Self-Help Law Books

Before using a self-help law book, you should realize the advantages and disadvantages of doing your own legal work and understand the challenges and diligence that this requires.

The Growing Trend

Rest assured that you will not be the first or only person handling your own legal matter. For example, in some states, more than 75% of divorces and other cases have at least one party representing him- or herself. Because of the high cost of legal services, this is a major trend and many courts are struggling to make it easier for people to represent themselves. However, some courts are not happy with people who do not use attorneys and refuse to help them in any way. For some, the attitude is, "Go to the law library and figure it out for yourself."

We write and publish self-help law books to give people an alternative to the often complicated and confusing legal books found in most law libraries. We have made the explanations of the law as simple and easy to understand as possible. Of course, unlike an attorney advising an individual client, we cannot cover every conceivable possibility.

Cost/Value Analysis

Whenever you shop for a product or service, you are faced with various levels of quality and price. In deciding what product or service to buy, you make a cost/value analysis on the basis of your willingness to pay and the quality you desire.

When buying a car, you decide whether you want transportation, comfort, status, or sex appeal. Accordingly, you decide among such choices as a Neon, Lincoln, Rolls Royce, or Porsche. Before making a decision, you usually weigh the merits of each option against the cost.

When you get a headache, you can take a pain reliever (such as aspirin) or visit a medical specialist for a neurological examination. Given this choice, most people, of course, take a pain reliever, since it costs only pennies, whereas a medical examination costs hundreds of dollars and takes a lot of time. This is usually a logical choice because it is rare to need anything more than a pain reliever for a headache. But in some cases, a headache may indicate a brain tumor and failing to see a specialist right away can result in complications. Should everyone with a headache go to a specialist? Of course not, but people treating their own illnesses must realize that they are betting on the basis of their cost/value analysis of the situation. They are taking the most logical option.

The same cost/value analysis must be made when deciding to do one's own legal work. Many legal situations are very straightforward, requiring a simple form and no complicated analysis. Anyone with a little intelligence and a book of instructions can handle the matter without outside help.

But there is always the chance that complications are involved that only an attorney would notice. To simplify the law into a book like this, several legal cases often must be condensed into a single sentence or paragraph. Otherwise, the book would be several hundred pages long and too complicated for most people. However, this simplification necessarily leaves out many details and nuances that would apply to special or unusual situations. Also, there are many ways to interpret most legal questions. Your case may come before a judge who disagrees with the analysis of our authors.

Therefore, in deciding to use a self-help law book and to do your own legal work, you must realize that you are making a cost/value analysis. You have decided that the money you will save in doing it yourself outweighs the chance that your case will not turn out to your satisfaction. Most people handling their own simple legal matters never have a problem, but occasionally people find that it ended up costing them more to have an attorney straighten out the situation than it would have if they had hired an attorney in the beginning.

Keep this in mind if you decide to handle your own case, and be sure to consult an attorney if you feel you might need further guidance.

Local Rules The next thing to remember is that a book that covers the law for the entire nation, or even for an entire state, cannot possibly include every procedural difference of every county court. Whenever possible, we provide the exact form needed; however, in some areas, each county, or even each judge, may require unique forms and procedures. In our state books, our forms usually cover the majority of counties in the state, or provide examples of the type of form that will be required. In our national books, our forms are sometimes even more general in nature, but are designed to give a good idea of the type of form that will be needed in most locations. Nonetheless, keep in mind that your state, county, or judge may have a requirement, or use a form, that is not included in this book.

You should not necessarily expect to be able to get all the information and resources you need solely from within the pages of this book. This book will serve as your guide, giving you specific information whenever possible and helping you to find out what else you will need to know. This is just like if you decided to build your own backyard deck. You might purchase a book on how to build decks. However, such a book would not include the building codes and permit requirements of every city, town, county, and township in the nation; nor would it include the lumber, nails, saws, hammers, and other materials and tools you would need to actually build the deck. You would use the book as your guide, and then do some work and research involving such matters as whether you need a permit of some kind, what type and grade of wood are available in your area, whether to use hand tools or power tools, and how to use those tools.

Before using the forms in a book like this, you should check with your court clerk to see if there are any local rules of which you should be aware, or local forms you will need to use. Often, such forms will require the same information as the forms in the book but are merely laid out differently, use slightly different language, or use different color paper so the clerks can easily find them. They will sometimes require additional information.

Changes in the Law

Besides being subject to state and local rules and practices, the law is subject to change at any time. The courts and the legislatures of all fifty states are constantly revising the laws. It is possible that while you are reading this book, some aspect of the law is being changed or that a court is interpreting a law in a different way. You should always check the most recent statutes, rules, and regulations to see what, if any, changes have been made.

In most cases, the change will be of minimal significance. A form will be redesigned, additional information will be required, or a waiting period will be extended. As a result, you might need to revise a form, file an extra form, or wait out a longer time period; these types of changes will not usually affect the outcome of your case. On the other hand, sometimes a major part of the law is changed, the entire law in a particular area is rewritten, or a case that was the basis of a central legal point is overruled. In such instances, your entire ability to pursue your case may be impaired.

Again, you should weigh the value of your case against the cost of an attorney and make a decision as to what you believe is in your best interest.

Introduction

THE PURPOSE OF THIS BOOK

This book has a broad application. It is intended to provide useful forms for all businesses, whatever their legal structure may be. Therefore, for businesses run as partnerships, sole proprietorships, corporations, or other forms, this book stands alone.

This book may decrease dependence on lawyers, but it may not in more complex cases. It will have served its purpose if it helps you to recognize the occasions in which you do need a lawyer, and then helps you to use your lawyer more efficiently.

Failing to hire a lawyer when you need one is not likely to be economical. If, in reading this book, you discover that what you want to do is more complicated than you imagined or involves a large sum of money, then get a lawyer. It would be better to pay for a lawyer, even if in the end you determine his or her services were unnecessary, rather than try to handle a complex matter for which you are unqualified on your own.

Use your lawyer's services wisely; do not leave everything up to him or her. You know your business and what is important for it. The best lawyer's ideas about your business may be completely wrong, and he or she may attach importance to the unimportant (because it was important to the last client) and gloss over a critical factor. Use this book to know what to expect from your lawyer and why. And then read and understand the work your lawyer does for you. Make sure it fits your situation.

The forms in this book have been limited to those that will be usable in all states. There are other business forms books on the market that claim to be comprehensive, but include many forms (such as deeds, bad check notices, and leases) that are unusable in many states. For example, deeds vary from state to state. Some states have very specific requirements for how the witnesses must be indicated, the form of the notary public certification, and where and how much space must be left blank for the entry of recording information.

In the past, each state had its own official form for filing a security interest under the Uniform Commercial Code (UCC-1 form), and some assessed penalties for failing to use the official form. The trend is toward standardized forms, which are the forms used in this book. However, you should always check your state law for any variation to the forms. Some states have specific forms for bad check notices, and have required statements and warnings in leases. It would be impossible to provide such forms for each state in a book such as this, and it would be irresponsible to include such forms knowing that they will not comply with the laws in every state.

In recent years, the federal and state governments have made great use of the Internet. Filing and research that used to require a visit to a courthouse or state government office can now be done from your desk. Most states, the Internal Revenue Service (IRS), and other agencies have posted downloadable forms online for your use.

ORGANIZATION OF THIS BOOK

The first chapter of the book deals with some general principles of contract law, and following chapters apply those principles to specific situations. Before you use any of the contract forms in this book, pay careful attention to Chapter 1, especially the information about the proper execution of contracts. Depending on the form of your business—corporation, partnership, sole proprietorship, etc.—and the form of business of the entity you contract with, you will need to insert the proper signature format to make sure the proper party executes the contract and does so correctly.

Chapters 2 through 4 deal with employees and various other kinds of agents. In Chapters 5 through 8, the book deals with specific business transactions—buying and selling, renting, and borrowing and lending money. Chapter 9 deals with issues of liability—and how to avoid it—in connection with contract disputes and other matters. The appendix contains several miscellaneous forms that may be useful in connection with all the matters covered elsewhere in the book.

The sample forms presented throughout the book are filled in with information for fictional businesses. The forms may be abbreviated or otherwise slightly different from the forms in the appendix in order to save space. However, the samples throughout are numbered according to the blank forms in the appendix for ease of use.

If you come across a sample numbered "1," it corresponds to blank form 1 in the appendix. If you see a sample numbered "1A" or "1B," both of these samples relate to form 1, but are different versions. If you see a sample with no number, that means that there is no corresponding blank form in the appendix.

The forms in the appendix are designed to be used as is, although you may need to modify them to meet your specific needs. As previously stated, those included in the appendix are the forms generally used.

APPLICABLE LAWS

This book is intended to be used throughout the United States, and the laws of no specific jurisdiction are cited or relied on in this text. While the laws of each state vary significantly, general principles of contract and agency apply in every state. However, it may be that your specific circumstances raise a legal issue unique to your jurisdiction. For that reason and others, competent legal advice is always desirable. At times, the need for a lawyer is explicitly mentioned in this book.

How Contracts Work

A contract is an agreement that becomes legally binding. The contract is a private law created by the parties to the agreement and applying only to them. Like other laws, public or private, a contract is enforceable in a court of law.

A "PRIVATE" KIND OF LAW

Somewhere in the archives of Canterbury Cathedral in England is a contract, called the Accord of Winchester, that has been in force for nearly a thousand years. It is signed by King William and Queen Maude and the Archbishops of Canterbury and York. It was a bad deal for York. It put Canterbury in charge, and York did not like it. But it is that way to this day, and nobody expects the contract to be terminated or breached. It is the law.

Even if you are not the king, when you agree to a contract, you create a law that applies to you and the other people who contract with you. It remains the law until you agree to change it, all the obligations created by the contract are fulfilled, or it becomes impossible to enforce for one reason or another. If you break the law by breaching the contract, the injured party (the one who did not breach) can bring in enforcement help by going to court. If the court finds that it has jurisdiction, it will interpret the contract and determine whether it has been breached. If it has, then the court will require compliance or compensation, by force if necessary.

ENFORCING CONTRACTS

Are all agreements legally enforceable contracts? Clearly, the answer to this question is no. If you and your best friend agree to have lunch, and your friend does not show up, has a contract been broken? Probably not. You would not expect a court to waste its time on such a trivial matter. But suppose you agreed to meet with your lawyer for lunch to discuss an important transaction, and he or she fails to make it. As a result of your misplaced reliance on the lawyer, you are seriously disadvantaged and lose money on the transaction. You may think you should receive damages from the lawyer because he or she failed to keep an important promise.

How will the court know that the first lunch date agreement was trivial and the second was important enough to justify the court's intervention? It will look for the basic requirements, or *elements*, of a contract. If all the elements are there, then there is a contract, and the court will enforce it. The court looks for the following three elements: voluntary agreement, consideration, and legality. (The second element, consideration, distinguishes the two lunch dates).

Voluntary Agreement

A *voluntary agreement* is created when one person makes an offer to another person, who accepts it. The parties must have *capacity* (that is, they are sane, sober, and old enough to know what they are doing) and must not be under duress or otherwise deluded.

Consideration

Consideration is something given in exchange for something else. That is, it is something bargained for. It could be money or other property, an act (such as mowing the lawn), or even a promise to do (or not to do) something. But it must be something, however great or trivial. Courts do not like to concern themselves with the value of consideration, given that fairness and value are entirely too subjective.

Example:

Only you know how much you are willing to pay for your favorite rock star's used handkerchief, and if you decide to trade your house for it, as long as the other elements are present, the court will not stand in your way—or save you from yourself.

Legality
As a matter of policy, the courts will not enforce contracts to do something that is illegal or, in the court's opinion, severely detrimental to the public.

Example:
If you pay someone to have your spouse eliminated, and the contracting party botches the job, do not expect the court to award damages to you.

The courts even go so far as to refuse to allow professionals to collect otherwise legitimate fees for services if their professional licenses are not in order. Courts have refused to help landlords collect rent while their rental properties are in violation of building codes. This "hands off" policy is no doubt desirable, but has far-reaching consequences.

Example:
Drug dealers cannot rely on the courts to enforce contracts for the sale of illicit drugs, and so must turn to alternative enforcement agents. This adds to the cost of drugs and attracts undesirable people into the recreational drug business.

Society must weigh the advantages against the costs of all its policy decisions.

GETTING IT IN WRITING
You will notice that *writing* is not one of the elements listed above. It could have been, at least for some contracts. Every state makes some contracts unenforceable by the courts unless the contracts are written down and signed by the party trying to avoid the deal. You will hear lawyers say such contracts are "within the *Statute of Frauds*." They are referring to a very old English statute that has been enacted in one form or another throughout the United States. As used by modern lawyers, the phrase has become misleading. It has come to refer to all contracts that must be in writing to be enforceable, not just the ones you will see listed in your state's version of the Statute of Frauds.

Common examples of contracts within the Statute are contracts for the sale of real property, promises to pay a debt owed by another person, and contracts that will take more than one year to complete.

But most contracts are enforceable even if they are not in writing. Therefore, the usual purpose of getting something in writing is not to make it valid and legally binding, but rather to make it easier to prove that something is true. In other words, the writing is evidence, to be used in court if necessary, that something actually happened—that a promise was actually made, or an event actually occurred.

The writing does not have to be elaborate. It may not even have to be signed to be useful. Sometimes it is enough to have a written statement that can be proven to have been made by a particular person. If someone makes a promise to you that you intend to rely on, get the promisor to write it down. If he or she will not, then you write it down, date it, and sign it. Later you can swear that you wrote it down at the time the promise was made and that your description of the promise was accurate. It is not ideal, but it may be a little better than nothing.

The two sample forms on pages 6–8 are simple ways to get things in writing. Sample form 1 is a simple **Contract** form. A blank form can be found in the appendix. (see form 1, p.119.) The sample on page 8 is a contract in the form of a letter. If you write another person a letter describing a bargain the two of you have reached, and the addressee of the letter returns a copy of the letter with his or her signed consent to the terms as stated in the letter, you have a written contract. (Notice the word *bargain* in the preceding sentence, which implies the existence of consideration and the other elements of a contract previously mentioned.)

This format is also used by people who want a written acknowledgment of some oral statement previously made by the addressee. Such an acknowledgment may not be a contract, but at least the signer admits that whatever was stated in the letter is true and correct.

Even if the other person does not sign a copy of your letter, if you send the letter by *certified mail, return receipt requested*, you will at least be able to prove that you put your agreement in writing and the other party received it. If the other party cannot prove he or she replied to your letter by denying the existence of any such agreement, a court may decide there was an agreement as you claim.

Form 1 in the appendix is designed to allow you to insert extra pages if needed. At the bottom of the first page is the notation: "Page 1 of _____ pages." If you only need the two pages contained in the appendix, fill in the blank with the number "2," and on the second page fill in this notation to read: "Page __2__ of __2__ pages."

If you need one or more extra pages, repeat this notation on each additional page. For example, if you need one extra page, the first page would indicate: "Page 1 of __3__ pages." The second page would read: "Page __2__ of __3__ pages." The last page would read: "Page __3__ of __3__ pages."

Another way to put in additional provisions, especially after you have typed up the initial agreement, is to use an *addendum*. There is a provision on the second page of form 1 where you can indicate that an addendum is attached. There is an **ADDENDUM TO CONTRACT** form in the appendix. (see form 2, p.121.) There is a space on form 2 to fill in a number for the addendum, as there may be more than one addendum attached to a contract.

In addition to a general contract form, the appendix contains two special types of contracts for specific situations. There is a contract for the sale of goods called a **SALES AGREEMENT** (see form 27, p.175), and a **CONSIGNMENT SALES AGREEMENT** (see form 28, p.177).

Sample of Form 1: Contract

CONTRACT

THIS AGREEMENT is entered into by and between __Scrupulous Corporation of America__ (hereafter referred to as __SCA__) and __American Computer Consulting, Inc.__ (hereafter referred to as __ACC__). In consideration of the mutual promises made in this agreement and other valuable consideration, the receipt and sufficiency of which is acknowledged, the parties agree as follows:

    1.   ACC will provide SCA with ten hours of computer consulting services during the period from October 19, 2008, through October 23, 2008.

    2.   ACC will provide SCA with up to five hours of follow-up and trouble-shooting computer services for a period of one year from the date of this agreement.

    3.   SCA will pay ACC the sum of $800.00 for the services described in paragraphs 1 and 2; to be paid $400.00 on October 19, 2008, and $400.00 upon completion of the initial ten hours of consulting services.

    4.   ACC will provide SCA with additional consulting and trouble-shooting computer services at the rate of $75.00 per hour for a period of one year from the date of this agreement.

Page 1 of __2__ pages

The following addenda, dated the same date as this agreement, are incorporated in, and made a part of, this agreement:

☒ None.

This agreement shall be governed by the laws of _____New York_____.

If any part of this agreement is adjudged invalid, illegal, or unenforceable, the remaining parts shall not be affected and shall remain in full force and effect.

This agreement shall be binding upon the parties, and upon their heirs, executors, personal representatives, administrators, and assigns. No person shall have a right or cause of action arising out of or resulting from this agreement except those who are parties to it and their successors in interest.

This instrument, including any attached exhibits and addenda, constitutes the entire agreement of the parties. No representations or promises have been made except those that are set out in this agreement. This agreement may not be modified except in writing signed by all the parties.

IN WITNESS WHEREOF the parties have signed this agreement under seal on _____October 12, 2008_____.

Scrupulous Corporation of America

Henry Hardy
_____
Henry Hardy, President

Calvin Collier
_____
Calvin Collier, Secretary

(Corporate Seal)

American Computer Consulting, Inc.

James C. Jones
_____
James C. Jones,
Vice President

Jackson C. Jones
_____
Jackson C. Jones, Secretary

(Corporate Seal)

Page __2__ of __2__ pages.

Sample: Simple Letter Contract

Scrupulous Corporation of America ——————————————————
400 West 61st Avenue, P.O. Box 19
New York, NY 10032

October 12, 2008

James C. Jones, Vice President
American Computer Consulting, Inc.
143 East 75th Avenue
New York, NY 10033

Re: Agreement for Computer Consulting Services

Dear Mr. Jones:

   This letter will confirm the understanding reached between you and the undersigned on October 12, 2008, regarding the matter described above. We have agreed as follows:

   1. ACC will provide SCA with ten hours of computer consulting services during the period from October 19, 2008, through October 23, 2008.

   2. ACC will provide SCA with up to five hours of follow-up and trouble-shooting computer services for a period of one year from the date of this agreement.

   3. SCA will pay ACC the sum of $800.00 for the services described in paragraphs 1 and 2; to be paid $400.00 on October 19, 2008, and $400.00 upon completion of the initial ten hours of consulting services.

   4. ACC will provide SCA with additional consulting and trouble-shooting computer services at the rate of $75.00 per hour for a period of one year from the date of this agreement.

   Enclosed is a copy of this letter. If you agree to the above understanding, please so indicate by supplying your signature in the space provided on the enclosed copy and return it to me at the above address.

                              Sincerely,

                              Henry Hardy
                              ———————————————
                              Henry Hardy, President

Consented to and agreed on ___*10/12/2008*___.

___*James C. Jones*___
James C. Jones, Vice President
American Computer Consulting, Inc.

SIGNATURES

The **Contract** and the letter agreement on the previous page, like all properly prepared contracts, have spaces for signatures. Signatures have an almost magical reputation in our society, and in fact, your signature is a serious matter. It may be evidence that you have agreed to be legally bound to a promise. You should not give it lightly, and you should certainly not give it unintentionally.

Example:

A corporation called Seascape Restaurants, Inc., operated a restaurant called the Magic Moment. Mr. Rosenberg was one-third owner and president of Seascape. Mr. Costas contracted to build a new entrance for the restaurant, and Rosenberg signed the contract. Under Rosenberg's signature was typed "Jeff Rosenberg, the Magic Moment." The contract did not refer to Seascape, and Costas knew nothing of Seascape's existence.

After a dispute over performance of the contract, Costas sued Rosenberg personally for breach of contract. Rosenberg replied that the corporation, not he, should be liable for the contract, since the corporation owned the restaurant. But the court disagreed. Since the builder had no way of knowing that Seascape was involved, he should be allowed to rely on Rosenberg's signature and Rosenberg's word that he would keep the promises made in the contract. For all Costas knew, Rosenberg and Magic Moment were one and the same.

Rosenberg may have thought he was signing the corporation's signature, but in fact he was signing his own. How can you tell the difference? The following forms are examples of various types of signatures. If you are signing a contract on behalf of a corporation or some other entity besides yourself, you must be certain that the context is clear or else risk Mr. Rosenberg's fate. Do not just put your signature on a line because it is there. Make sure the document fits the situation; do not try to make the signature fit the preprinted document.

The law is actually flexible about what constitutes a signature. Whatever you put on a piece of paper, intending it to be your signature, will be sufficient. You may write someone else's name or someone else may write your name, but if you intend it to be your signature—and this intent can be proven in court—then it is your signature. Courts have recognized signatures written in the wrong place on the paper, and various kinds of marks other than names. The question is: what was your intent?

Signature of an Individual

The proper method for an individual's signature on a contract is found in the following sample signature. This is a signature *under seal*. In this case, the signer's seal is the word *seal* at the end of the signature line. No rubber stamp or gob of wax is required.

In some states, signing a document under seal is of little consequence, and it is rare that a document must be under seal in order to be valid and enforceable (often, however, real estate deeds must be under seal).

In some states, seals do have an important consequence. A seal may make it easier to prove the validity of the contract in court, or it may lengthen the time you have to enforce the contract in court (the *statute of limitations*). (To cover those states or situations where it may be important, the word "seal" will be used in many of the examples in this book.)

The use of the word *seal* by itself may not be enough. Some states require that the body of the contract refer to the parties' intent that the contract be under seal. Hence the sentence below the following sample signatures.

Sample Signature of an Individual

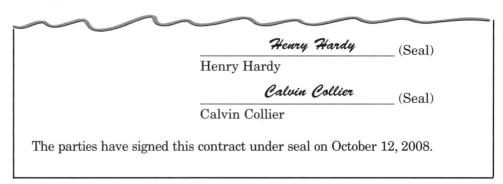

_____ _Henry Hardy_ _____ (Seal)
Henry Hardy

_____ _Calvin Collier_ _____ (Seal)
Calvin Collier

The parties have signed this contract under seal on October 12, 2008.

Signature of a Sole Proprietor

The signature of a sole proprietorship is really the same as an individual's signature, because the owner of the business operates it as an individual rather than as a separate entity. But if the business is conducted under a *trade name* (or *fictitious* or *assumed* name), confusion may result. The sample signature of a sole proprietorship business, shown next, makes it clear that the signature is that of a sole proprietor rather than a corporation or some other business organization. The letters *d/b/a* stand for *doing business as*. In its place, you may sometimes see *t/a* for *transacting as*.

Sample Signature of a Sole Proprietorship Business

_____ (Seal)
Henry Hardy
Henry Hardy, a sole proprietor
d/b/a Scrupulous Enterprises

Signatures of Corporations

Like individuals, corporations can sign documents under seal or not. The corporate seal usually carries somewhat more meaning than an individual's. In addition to the effects of an individual's seal previously mentioned, the corporate seal entitles other parties to the agreement to presume that the signer acted under the appropriate authorization of the corporation's board of directors. Corporate seals are usually rubber stamps or embossers, but anything the corporation's board of directors adopts by resolution as the corporate seal will do. The sample corporate signature (one officer) shows the signature of a corporation not under seal, and the sample corporate signature (under seal) shows that of a corporation under seal.

NOTE: *The secretary of the corporation in the sample corporate signature (under seal) is the custodian of the seal and is responsible for attesting that the president or vice president's signature is affixed by the board's authority.*

Sample Corporate Signature (One Officer)

Scrupulous Corporation

By: _____
Henry Hardy
Henry Hardy, President

Sample Corporate Signature (Under Seal)

This [document] is signed by the corporation under seal by authority of its board of directors on the <u>12</u> day of <u>October</u>, 20 <u>08</u>.

Scrupulous Corporation

By: *Henry Hardy*

Henry Hardy, President

(Corporate Seal)

Attest: *Calvin Collier*

Calvin Collier, Secretary

Signatures of General Partnerships

It may be helpful to think of a partnership as a group of sole proprietors in business together, where each member of the group acts as the agent of all the others. It is fundamental to partnership law that each partner is bound by the acts of the others in furtherance of the business and that each partner is liable for the debts of the partnership. It used to be that the law refused to recognize the partnership as an entity separate from the partners. This meant, for example, that a real estate deed for partnership property had to be signed by all the partners.

The modern rule, which is followed by the *Uniform Partnership Act*, the *Revised Uniform Partnership Act* (one of these has been enacted in all states except Louisiana), and the *Louisiana Partnership Act*, recognizes the separate existence of the partnership and holds that one partner, acting within his or her authority, can bind the rest of the partners on most contracts, including deeds.

This does not solve all the problems. Many states do not require general partnerships to publish lists of partners or explanations of the limits of their authority. It is not always possible to tell who is a partner or what limits there may be on a signer's authority. For this reason, persons entering into agreements with general partners should take precautions to make sure that the person signing has adequate authority. Sometimes all the partners will be asked to sign a document even though it may not be strictly required by the law to make a contract enforceable. You should have a written **PARTNERSHIP AGREEMENT**. A very simple agreement is provided in the appendix. (see form 16, p.151.)

You may see the initials *LLP* or *RLLP* after the name of a partnership. It means that the partnership is a *limited liability partnership* or a *registered limited liability partnership* (which is not the same as a *limited partnership*, described in the next section). A partner in an LLP is protected from certain liabilities. The extent and nature of the protection varies considerably from state to state. Limited liability partnerships are usually law firms or other professional organizations.

Example:

A lawyer in a law firm organized as an LLP will not be liable for the legal malpractice committed by another partner in the firm unless the malpractice was committed under the supervision of the first lawyer.

A sample general partnership signature follows. It shows the signature of a partnership, where one of the general partners has signed for the partnership.

Sample General Partnership Signature

Scrupulous Associates, a general partnership

By: ___*Henry Hardy*_____ (Seal)

Henry Hardy, General Partner

Signatures of Limited Partnerships

A *limited partnership* is much like a general partnership except that in addition to general partners, it has a special category of *limited partners* who do not participate in the management of the business and are not liable for the debts and liabilities of the business beyond the amount of their investment or *contribution*. A limited partnership is created under a special state statute, usually the *Uniform Limited Partnership Act*, and will have the words *limited partnership* or *LP* as part of its name.

Only a general partner (there may be one or more) will have authority to sign contracts, and limited partners usually have no authority to sign contracts for, or otherwise represent, the limited partnership. To add to the confusion, some states now recognize *registered limited liability limited partnerships* (RLLLP). Like the general partners in a limited liability partnership, the general partners in an RLLLP are protected from certain liabilities. RLLLP limited partners also enjoy limited liability.

Sample Limited Partnership Signature

Scrupulous Hardy Enterprises, a limited partnership

By: _*Henry Hardy*_____ (Seal)

Henry Hardy, General Partner

Signatures of Limited Liability Companies

A relatively new form of business called the *limited liability company* (LLC) has rapidly gained popularity. It combines the limited liability of corporations (that is, the company's owners are not personally liable for the debts and obligations of the LLC) with the tax attributes of a general partnership. The owners of LLCs are usually called *members*, and the people who run the company are called *managers*. The managers may have the powers usually associated with corporate directors and corporate officers, but, in some LLCs, management powers may be delegated to persons with titles corresponding to corporate titles, such as president, vice president, etc., or some other title.

A document may be signed on behalf of an LLC by a manager or some other person authorized to do so. If you have doubts about the authority of a person signing on behalf of an LLC, you may rely on an annual report filed by the LLC with the secretary of state, listing the managers of the company. The company's *operating agreement* may delegate authority to sign a document to a president or some other agent of the LLC. A manager will be willing to give a written certification of the authenticity of the terms of the company's operating agreement.

Sample Limited Liability Company Signature

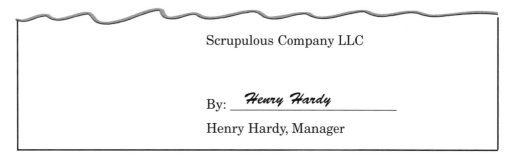

Scrupulous Company LLC

By: *Henry Hardy*

Henry Hardy, Manager

Other Signatures

Occasionally you run across types of businesses and charitable entities other than the ones already mentioned. For example, you may see the initials PC, PLP, or PLLC following a company or partnership name. These are *professional corporations*, *limited partnerships*, and *professional limited liability companies*. They differ from ordinary businesses in that the owners do not enjoy the same degree of limited liability as the owners of ordinary companies and partnerships, but the rules about signatures are the same.

NOTARIES AND ACKNOWLEDGMENTS

A notary public is empowered by the state to administer various oaths and to testify to the genuineness of signatures. The term *acknowledgment* refers to a signer's statement that he or she truly is the person signing the document, and that (in the case of a corporate officer) he or she holds the corporate office claimed. The notary will verify the identity of the signer and affirm in writing that the person signing the document is who he or she claims to be. Notaries public are bound by very strict rules imposed by state law. A notary may not notarize a signature unless the document was signed in the notary's presence, or the signer—while in the notary's presence—affirms that he or she signed the document. The notary must ask for suitable identification unless the notary personally knows the signer. A notary who violates these rules may be subject to civil or even criminal penalties.

Frequently, state statutes provide specific notarization forms for documents such as deeds, car titles, and oaths of office.

Sample Acknowledgment by an Individual

STATE OF TEXAS   )
COUNTY OF HOCKLEY   )

     I certify that _____Henry Hardy_____, who ☒ is personally known to me to be the person whose name is subscribed to the foregoing instrument ❑ produced _____ _____ as identification, personally appeared before me on __September 6, 2008__, and ☒ acknowledged the execution of the foregoing instrument ❑ acknowledged that (s)he is (Assistant) Secretary of _____ and that by authority duly given and as the act of the corporation, the foregoing instrument was signed in its name by its (Vice) President, sealed with its corporate seal, and attested by him/her as its (Assistant) Secretary.

_____
Notary Public, State of Texas
My commission expires: Sept. 30, 2010

Sample Acknowledgment by a Corporation

STATE OF TEXAS   )
COUNTY OF HOCKLEY   )

     I certify that _____Calvin Collier_____, who ❑ is personally known to me to be the person whose name is subscribed to the foregoing instrument ☒ produced ___Texas Drivers Lic.___ as identification, personally appeared before me on __September 6, 2008__, and ❑ acknowledged the execution of the foregoing instrument ☒ acknowledged that (s)he is (~~Assistant~~) Secretary of __Scrupulous Corporation of America__, and that by authority duly given and as the act of the corporation, the foregoing instrument was signed in its name by its (~~Vice~~) President, sealed with its corporate seal, and attested by him/~~her~~ as its (~~Assistant~~) Secretary.

_____
Notary Public, State of Texas
My commission expires: Sept. 30, 2010

AMENDING A CONTRACT

Sometimes the parties to a contract will come to the conclusion that the contract no longer reflects their agreement and needs to be modified. Unless otherwise agreed in the original contract, the modification of a contract is a contract in its own right and must contain all the elements described earlier in this chapter, including consideration. The sample of form 3 on page 18 is a general form for amending an existing contract. A blank **AMENDMENT TO CONTRACT** is in the appendix.

(see form 3, p.123.) (Also see sample of form 44 on page 225, which is a form for amending a lease.)

There is an exception to the rule that a contract amendment, or *contract to change a contract*, must be supported by consideration. If it is a contract for the sale of goods (as opposed to a contract for services or a lease of real property, for example), the Uniform Commercial Code (UCC), which is the statute that governs such contracts, says that it does not have to be supported by new consideration.

Example:

A merchant agrees to sell a dozen tires at $75 per tire. The merchant and the buyer then agree that $75 is too high a price and that the purchase price should be only $70 per tire. Under the common law of contracts, that amendment to the contract would have to be supported by consideration. The merchant might say, "I'll reduce the price per tire to $70 if you will agree to pick up the tires at my warehouse rather than requiring me to deliver the tires to your garage."

Under common law contract rules, without the new consideration regarding the shipment terms, the original $75 price would prevail, and the buyer would have to pay. Under the UCC, the details about changing the terms of delivery would not be necessary to make the price reduction enforceable.

Treat this rule with care. All contracts governed by the Uniform Commercial Code include an implied promise to act in good faith. If a party agrees to a change in the terms of a contract because he or she is unfairly forced into doing so, the courts may refuse to enforce the change in any case.

Example:

Suppose you agree to sell sugar to a doughnut baker at an agreed-upon price. You know that the baker has no other readily available source of sugar, so you decide to raise the price you have agreed to. The baker is forced to go along (or else, no doughnuts) and agrees to the higher price under the UCC rule. Later, the baker refuses to pay the higher price, relying on the original terms of the contract. A court would be likely to say the baker's agreement to raise the price is unenforceable, because the sugar seller acted in bad faith.

Sample of Form 3: Amendment to Contract

AMENDMENT TO CONTRACT

For valuable consideration, the receipt and sufficiency of which is acknowledged by each of the parties, this agreement amends a Contract dated __October 12,__ , __2008__ between __Scrupulous Corporation of America__ and __American Computer Consulting, Inc.__ , relating to __computer consulting services__ . This contract amendment is hereby incorporated into the Contract.

Paragraph 1 is amended to read as follows:

1. ACC will provide SCA with ten hours of computer consulting services during the period from October 19, 2008, through November 1, 2008.

Except as changed by this amendment, the Contract shall continue in effect according to its terms. The amendments herein shall be effective on the date this document is executed by all parties.

Executed on _____October 21, 2008_____ .

Scrupulous Corporation of America

Henry Hardy

Henry Hardy, President

Calvin Collier

Calvin Collier, Secretary
(Corporate Seal)

American Computer Consulting, Inc.

James C. Jones

James C. Jones, Vice President

Jackson C. Jones

Jackson C. Jones, Secretary
(Corporate Seal)

ASSIGNING A CONTRACT

The right to performance under a contract is a property right like any other and ordinarily can be bought and sold. Courts distinguish between the *assignment* of your right to receive performance from the other party, and the *delegation* of your duty to perform a contractual promise.

Example:

If you are the landlord under an apartment rental agreement, you can assign the right to receive the monthly rent payments to another party, without delegating your duty to maintain the property. If you are the tenant, you can delegate your duty to pay rent to a replacement tenant (as well as assign your right to live in the apartment). (see Chapter 5.)

The difference is that after you *assign* your rights, you do not have them any more; but after you *delegate* your duties, you may not be entirely rid of them. If the substitute tenant fails to pay the rent, the landlord will still be able to collect from you. (However, the written terms of the rental agreement may alter these basic legal rules.)

There are some exceptions to the rule that contract rights and duties can be assigned or delegated. For one thing, the parties to a contract may specifically agree that no such assignment or delegation is permitted. The nature of some contracts makes the rights and duties nontransferrable.

Example:

Suppose you hire a famous opera singer to sing at your birthday party. Just before the party, the singer calls to say that he does not feel like singing and has delegated his duty to sing to his chauffeur. You would reasonably object that you hired the famous singer to do the job, not his driver. The courts would agree, because the singer's performance is *personal* to the contract. No one else will do.

Many people use the term *contract assignment* to mean both the assignment of rights and the delegation of duties. However, if you intend to delegate a duty, it is better to be specific. If you wish to rid yourself of the possibility of ever having to perform the duty, you must be released from that duty by the person entitled to receive the performance.

An example of an **ASSIGNMENT OF CONTRACT** is provided as follows as a sample. The blank form is in the appendix. (see form 4, p.125.)

Sample of Form 4: Assignment of Contract

ASSIGNMENT OF CONTRACT

FOR VALUE RECEIVED the undersigned (the "Assignor") hereby assigns, transfers, and conveys to _____Bartholomew Simpson, d/b/a B.S. Painting_____ (the "Assignee") all the Assignor's rights, title, and interests in and to a contract (the "Contract") dated ___August 3, 2008___, between _____the Assignor_____ and _____Fred's Appliance Warehouse, Inc._____.

The Assignor hereby warrants and represents that the Contract is in full force and effect and is fully assignable.

The Assignee hereby assumes the duties and obligations of the Assignor under the Contract and agrees to hold the Assignor harmless from any claim or demand thereunder.

The date of this assignment is ___August 8, 2008___.

IN WITNESS WHEREOF this assignment is signed by the parties under seal.

Assignor: Assignee:

Acme Painters, Inc.

By: ___*Robert Sherwyn*___   ___*Bartholomew Simpson*___ (seal)
Robert Sherwyn, President   Bartholomew Simpson,
                                                               d/b/a B.S. Painting

---

Having assigned a contract, it is important to notify the person expecting to receive the performance that the assignment has been made.

Example:

Suppose the assigned contract is an agreement to move one hundred cases of wine from warehouse A to warehouse B. Quick Moving Co. assigns the moving contract to Fast Movers, Inc., which promptly does the job, but neglects to notify the owner of the wine that the contract has been assigned. The owner arrives at warehouse B, discovers the job complete, and sends a check for the moving job to Quick Moving. Fast Movers then asks to be paid. Fast Movers cannot recover its fee from the owner, because the owner has performed his part of the contract, paying for the completed job, as required by the terms of the agreement. Fast Movers will have to hope it can recover the fee from Quick Moving. If Fast Movers had promptly notified the owner of the assignment, then the owner would have paid Fast Movers directly.

The sample notice of assignment of a contract that follows is an example of the type of letter that would have helped Fast Movers in the previous example. It may be used to notify someone that the sender has assumed the duty to perform some service, and that payment should therefore be sent to the new person performing the service.

Frequently, the contract being assigned is the right to receive payment for a debt. See the sample in Chapter 8, on page 93, for a notice to the debtor that future payments should be made to the assignee of the debt.

Sample Notice of Assignment of a Contract

B.S. Painting
8321 S. Main Street
Fort Worth, TX 76011

September 8, 2008

Fred Jackson, President
Fred's Appliance Warehouse, Inc.
842 US Highway 81
Fort Worth, TX 76012

Dear Mr. Jackson:

We are pleased to inform you that we have assumed the duties of Acme Painters, Inc., pursuant to a contract dated September 3, 2008, in which Acme Painters, Inc., agreed to paint your building at 842 US Highway 81, Fort Worth, Texas.

Any questions you may have, and all payments due from you pursuant to the contract, should be directed to the undersigned at the address given above.

Sincerely,

Bartholomew Simpson

Bartholomew Simpson, d/b/a
B.S. Painting

TERMINATING CONTRACTS

Contracts are terminated for different reasons and under different circumstances. One is that all the parties to a contract have completely performed the duties they had to perform according to its terms. But suppose that, before the parties completely perform their duties, they decide to call it off. The following sample is the basic language for an agreement between two parties to terminate a contract and release each other from all duties to be performed.

Sample of Form 6: Termination of an Agreement by Consent of the Parties

---

TERMINATION OF CONTRACT

Date: _____9/12/08_____

The undersigned have entered into a contract dated _____September 3, 2008_____ (the "Contract") for the purpose of:

painting a building

The undersigned acknowledge that, by their mutual agreement, the Contract is hereby terminated without further recourse by either party.

The termination of the Contract shall be effective on (date) September 12, 2008 .

Breach   Another way for a contract to be terminated is for one or more parties to breach the agreement so completely that the other parties are relieved of their duties to perform.

Example:

If you contract to have your house painted and the painter completely fails to perform the job, then you are relieved of your promise to pay.

Most breaches are not so clear-cut, of course. Usually if one party believes the other is not living up to its duties, the party in default will be notified of its shortcomings and a period of negotiation and compromise will follow. The sample listed next is a notice given by one party to another that the latter is not living up to a promise.

Sample of Form 5: Notice of Breach of Contract

NOTICE OF BREACH OF CONTRACT

September 12, 2008

To: Bartholomew Simpson, d/b/a B.S. Painting

Dear Sir,

We refer to a contract dated _____September 3, 2008_____ (the "Contract") pursuant to which you have obligated yourself to _paint our entire building_ .

You have breached your duties under the Contract in that you have failed to _paint the south wall_.

We demand that you cure such default promptly. In the event that you fail to do so within seven days of the date of this letter, we will refer the matter to attorneys for immediate action.

Sincerely,

Fred Jackson

Fred Jackson, President
Fred's Appliance Warehouse, Inc.

Employees

This chapter discusses various aspects of having employees. Matters concerning independent contractors are covered in Chapter 3. There is an **APPLICATION FOR EMPLOYMENT** in the appendix that can be used either alone or with an applicant's resumé. (see form 7, p.131.) The information obtained can be useful in comparing applicants and checking employment history. In hiring employees, it is a good idea to develop some kind of ranking criteria so that you can justify your hiring decisions if you are ever confronted with a charge of illegal discrimination by an unsuccessful applicant.

An important matter not to be overlooked is being sure your prospective employee is legally eligible to work in the United States. There is an **EMPLOYMENT ELIGIBILITY VERIFICATION (IRS FORM I-9)** required by the federal government. The form includes instructions. (see form 9, p.135.)

EMPLOYMENT CONTRACTS

It is not necessary to have a written employment contract. However, contracts for employment that cannot be completed within a year may not be enforceable unless they are in writing. Some businesses have a policy against employment contracts and hire their employees *at will*, meaning that they can be fired or can quit at any time. But often the law limits the conditions under which even an at will employee can be fired.

The first sample of form 8, on the following page, is a simple **EMPLOYMENT AGREEMENT** for a permanent, salaried employee. (see form 8, p.133.) The other samples of form 8, on the subsequent pages, show how different pertinent sections of the contract would be completed for various other types of employment situations.

Sample of Form 8: Employment Contract for a *Salaried Employee*

EMPLOYMENT AGREEMENT

This employment agreement is entered into by and between _____
__Leona Halsey_____(the "Employee") and _____
__Southern Hotel Supply, Inc._____ (the "Employer"), who agree as fol-
lows:

1. The Employer has hired the Employee to fill the following position:
   Account and Billing Supervisor

☒ See attached description.

2. Term. The term of Employee's employment shall begin on __October 7, 2008__. Employment pursuant to this agreement shall be "at will" and may be ended by the Employee or by the Employer at any time and for any reason. This is an agreement for employment that is:

☒ permanent, but "at will."

☐ temporary, but "at will," _____

_____.

3. Probation. It is understood that the first ___60___ days of employment shall be probationary only and that if the Employee's services are not satisfactory to the Employer, employment shall
be terminated at the end of this probationary period.

4. Compensation and Benefits. The Employee's compensation and benefits during the term of
this agreement shall be as stated in this paragraph, and may be adjusted from time to time by the
Employer. Initially, the Employer shall pay the Employee:

☒   a salary in the amount of _____$19,240 per year_____,
payable _____at the rate of $370 each week_____.

☐ an hourly wage of $_____ , payable _____.

☐ a commission of _____% of _____.
In addition to such commission, the Employee shall receive _____
_____.

☒   the following benefits: _____Employer will provide group health insurance_____
                        __after successful completion of probationary period_____.

☐   other:

5. Work Hours. The hours and schedule worked by the Employee may be adjusted from time to
time by the Employer. Initially, the Employee shall work the following hours each week:
   9:00 a.m. to 5:00 p.m., Monday through Friday.

6. Additional Terms. The Employee also agrees to the terms of the attached:

   ☐ No other agreements are attached   ☐ Confidentiality Agreement

❏ Agreement on Patents and Inventions   ☒ Indemnification Agreement

❏ Other:_____

7. This agreement shall be governed by the laws of _____Florida_____.

8. It is the Employer's intention to comply with all federal, state, and local laws that apply to the business, including, but not limited to, labor, equal opportunity, privacy, and sexual harassment laws. The Employee shall promptly report to the Employer any violations encountered in the business. The Employee shall at all time comply with any and all federal, state, and local laws.

9. The Employee shall not have the power to make any contracts or commitments on behalf of the Employer without the express written consent of the Employer.

10. In the event one party fails to insist upon performance of a part of this agreement, such failure shall not be construed as waiving those terms, and this entire agreement shall remain in full force.

11. In the event a dispute of any nature arises between the parties to this agreement, the parties agree to submit the dispute to binding arbitration under the rules of the American Arbitration Association. An award rendered by the arbitrator(s) shall be final and binding upon the parties and judgment on such award may be entered by either party in the highest court having jurisdiction. Each party specifically waives his or her right to bring the dispute before a court of law and stipulates that this agreement shall be a complete defense to any action instituted in any local, state, or federal court or before any administrative tribunal.

12. If any part of this agreement is adjudged invalid, illegal, or unenforceable, the remaining parts shall not be affected and shall remain in full force and effect.

13. This agreement shall be binding upon the parties, and upon their heirs, executors, personal representatives, administrators, and assigns. No person shall have a right or cause of action arising out of or resulting from this agreement except those who are parties to it and their successors in interest.

14. This instrument, including any attached agreements specified in paragraph 6 above, constitutes the entire agreement of the parties. No representations or promises have been made except those that are set out in this agreement. This agreement may not be modified except in writing signed by all the parties.

15. IN WITNESS WHEREOF the parties have signed this agreement under seal on _____October 7, 2008_____.

Employer: Employee:
Southern Hotel Supply, Inc.

By _*Jake Southern*_____   _*Leona Halsey*_____(Seal)
    Jake Southern, President   Leona Halsey

Sample of Form 8: Portion of Employment Contract for a *Commissioned Employee*

4.   Compensation and Benefits. The Employee's compensation and benefits during the term of this agreement shall be as stated in this paragraph, and may be adjusted from time to time by the Employer. Initially, the Employer shall pay the Employee:

☐ a salary in the amount of _____ , payable

_____ .

☐ an hourly wage of $_____ , payable _____ .

☒ a commission of __5__ % of _____ gross sales receipts _____ .

   In addition to such commission, the Employee shall receive _____

   _____ an expense account of $100 per week _____ .

☒ the following benefits: __ group medical and dental insurance coverage _____

_____ .

☐ other:

Sample of Form 8: Portion of Employment Contract for a *Part-Time Employee (Hourly Wage)*

5.   Work Hours. The hours and schedule worked by the Employee may be adjusted from time to time by the Employer. Initially, the Employee shall work the following hours each week:

8:00 a.m. to 12:30 p.m., on Mondays, Wednesdays, and Fridays.

Sample of Form 8: Portion of Employment Contract for a *Temporary Employee*

2.   Term. The term of Employee's employment shall begin on _____ October 7, 2008 _____ . Employment pursuant to this agreement shall be "at will" and may be ended by the Employee or by the Employer at any time and for any reason. This is an agreement for employment that is:

☐   permanent, but "at will."

☒   temporary, but "at will," _____ for the period of October 7, 2008, to _____

_____ January 4, 2009, at such times and on such dates as needed _____ .

The Officer as Employee

An officer is always an agent of the corporation, but it is not always true that an officer is an employee of the corporation.

Example:

An officer may be the employee of a parent corporation, who serves as an officer of a subsidiary as a convenience to the employer parent. Or the corporation may be a small family company where a spouse serves as secretary or assistant secretary as a convenience to the person who runs the business.

Where the officer is an employee, it may be desirable to have a written employment contract.

RESIGNATION AND TERMINATION

At will employees serve at the pleasure of the employer, subject to certain state and federal regulations. An **EMPLOYMENT AGREEMENT** may be for a specific term, but that does not mean the employer must keep an employee he or she does not want. However, depending on the employment contract, the employer could be liable for damages to the employee as a result of such termination. Similarly, an employee with such a contract could resign at any time, but if the resignation is in breach of the agreement, the employee could be liable for damages.

An employee's resignation can be as simple as a letter addressed to the employer (possibly to the employee's supervisor or the person who hired him or her), stating something like, "I hereby resign my employment as packaging manager, effective March 31, 2008, at 5:00 p.m." It should be dated and signed by the employee. To make it final and irreversible, it is a good idea for the employer to give the employee a letter accepting his or her resignation.

SPECIAL EMPLOYMENT AGREEMENTS

Confidentiality

Often an employee will learn information about the business that the employer wants kept secret. A **CONFIDENTIALITY AGREEMENT** creates a contractual obligation to keep the secret. (see form 10, p.139.) If the secret is revealed, the employee will be liable to the employer for damages resulting from the breach. In the case of trade secrets and other important matters, the damages the employee is capable of paying may be far less than the actual damages incurred, so it is best not to rely too much on such an agreement. Give employees information on a need to know basis if possible, and hire employees you can trust.

Ideally, a confidentiality agreement should be made a part of the employment agreement. Often an employer will not think of the need for a **CONFIDENTIALITY AGREEMENT** until after an employee is hired. This oversight leads to a common problem: The employer will ask the employee to give his or her promise of confidentiality, but the employer may give nothing in exchange for it. The confidentiality agreement will therefore lack consideration (see page 2) and will be legally unenforceable. A promise by the employer to continue the employee's employment may not be enough to provide consideration, because the employee may already have the right to continued employment. Form 10 in the appendix (p.139) allows for additional consideration such as cash, a raise in salary, or an extension of the terms of employment beyond that already provided.

Sample of Form 10: Confidentiality Agreement

CONFIDENTIALITY AGREEMENT

This agreement is made between _____Lamar Leakey_____ (the "Employee") and
_____Scrupulous Corporation_____ (the "Employer").

The Employee agrees to the terms of this agreement:

☐ contemporaneously with and as part of the terms of the Employment Agreement by which the Employee is being hired by the Employer which Employment Agreement is incorporated by reference.

☒ in consideration of the Employee's continued employment by the Employer and additional consideration consisting of ___the sum of $1,000.00 (One thousand and 00/100 dollars)___, which the Employee acknowledges is sufficient consideration paid by the Employer over and above the consideration due to the Employee pursuant to his or her usual terms of employment.

1. The Employee acknowledges that, in the course of employment by the Employer, the Employee has, and may in the future, come into the possession of certain confidential information belonging to the Employer including, but not limited to, trade secrets, customer lists, supplier lists and prices, pricing schedules, methods, processes, or marketing plans.

2. The Employee hereby covenants and agrees that he or she will at no time, during or after the term of employment, use for his or her own benefit or the benefit of others, or disclose or divulge to others, any such confidential information.

3. Upon termination of employment, the Employee will return to the Employer, retaining no copies, all documents relating to the Employer's business including, but not limited to, reports, manuals, drawings, diagrams, blueprints, correspondence, customer lists, computer programs, and all other materials and all copies of such materials, obtained by the Employee during employment.

4. Violation of this agreement by the Employee will entitle the Employer to an injunction to prevent such competition or disclosure (posting of any bond by the Employer is hereby waived), and will entitle the Employer to other legal remedies, including attorney's fees and costs.

5. This agreement shall be governed by the laws of __North Carolina__.

6. If any part of this agreement is adjudged invalid, illegal, or unenforceable, the remaining parts shall not be affected and shall remain in full force and effect.

7. This agreement shall be binding upon the parties, and upon their heirs, executors, personal representatives, administrators, and assigns. No person shall have a right or cause of action arising out of or resulting from this agreement except those who are parties to it and their successors in interest.

8. This instrument, including any attached exhibits and addenda, constitutes the entire agreement of the parties. No representations or promises have been made except those that are set out in this agreement. This agreement may not be modified except in writing signed by all the parties.

IN WITNESS WHEREOF the parties have signed this agreement under seal on __7/10/08__.

Employer: Employee:

_____   _____

_____   _____

Patents, Inventions, Copyrights, Etc.

Another fruitful area for disputes is where an employee creates a patentable invention or copyrightable material. The question becomes: who owns it, the employer or the employee? Without a specific agreement, a court may have to decide, considering such matters as the employee's job description, the nature of the invention or material, and whether it was created on company time and using company resources.

An **EMPLOYEE'S AGREEMENT ON PATENTS AND INVENTIONS** designed to provide protection for the employer is included in the appendix. (see form 11, p.141.) Forms 14, 48, and 49 can be used for either an employee or a non-employee to commission an artist or author to create a specific work. You can obtain all rights to the work with the **WORK MADE-FOR-HIRE AGREEMENT**. (see form 14, p.147.) You can acquire the copyrights in an existing work with the **ASSIGNMENT OF COPYRIGHT**. (see form 48, p.233.) Finally, where the owner of a copyright is willing to authorize you to use his or her copyrighted work for certain purposes, but is not willing to give up all rights, you can use the **COPYRIGHT LICENSE**. (see form 49, p.235.)

Sample of Form 11: Employee's Agreement on Patents and Inventions

---

EMPLOYEE'S AGREEMENT ON PATENTS AND INVENTIONS

This agreement is made between _____Carlin Ventor_____ (the "Employee") and __Scrupulous Corporation__ (the "Employer").

The Employee agrees to the terms of this agreement:

☐ contemporaneously with and as part of the terms of the Employment Agreement by which the Employee is being hired by the Employer which Employment Agreement is incorporated by reference.

☒ in consideration of the Employee's continued employment by the Employer and additional consideration consisting of _____, which the Employee acknowledges is sufficient consideration paid by the Employer over and above the consideration due to the Employee pursuant to his or her usual terms of employment.

1. During the term of the Employee's employment and for a period of __12__ months thereafter, the Employee will promptly and completely disclose and assign to the Employer every invention, product, process, mechanism, or design that the Employee may invent, create, develop, or discover that in any way relates to, or may be suggested by, the Employer's business or the Employee's employment duties. Such disclosure or assignment shall be made free of any obligation by the Employer to the Employee and without the necessity of any further request by the Employer.

2. The Employee will, at the Employer's expense, cooperate with the Employer in applying for and securing in the name of the Employer patents with respect to the matters required to be disclosed pursuant to this agreement in each country where the Employer wishes to secure such patents. Without limiting the foregoing, the Employee will promptly execute all proper documents presented to him or her for signature by the Employer in connection with the securing of such patents and the transfer of such patents to the Employer and will give such true information and testimony, under oath if so requested, as the Employer may reasonably require in connection with such matters.

3. The following is a complete list of all inventions, applications for patent, and patents in which the Employee holds an interest, and which are not subject to this agreement:

4. This agreement shall be governed by the laws of __North Carolina__.

5. If any part of this agreement is adjudged invalid, illegal, or unenforceable, the remaining parts shall not be affected and shall remain in full force and effect.

6. This agreement shall be binding upon the parties, and upon their heirs, executors, personal representatives, administrators, and assigns. No person shall have a right or cause of action arising out of or resulting from this agreement except those who are parties to it and their successors in interest.

7. This instrument, including any attached exhibits and addenda, constitutes the entire agreement of the parties. No representations or promises have been made except those that are set out in this agreement. This agreement may not be modified except in writing signed by all the parties.

IN WITNESS WHEREOF the parties have signed this agreement under seal on ___10/30/08___.

Employer: Employee:

_____   _____

_____   _____

Sample of Form 14: Work Made-For-Hire Agreement

WORK MADE-FOR-HIRE AGREEMENT

This Agreement is made this __10th__ day of ____July____, __2008__, between __Scrupulous__ __Corporation__ as Owner, and ____Elizabeth R. Tiste____ as Author/Artist.

WHEREAS the Owner wishes to commission a Work called _"Homage to Scrupulousness"_ and;

WHEREAS the Author/Artist has represented that he/she can create said work according to the specifications provided by the Owner;

It is agreed between the parties hereto that in consideration of the sum of $____175,000.00____, to be paid by the Owner to the Author/Artist within thirty days of satisfactory completion of the work, the Author/Artist shall create the Work as specified. Upon payment, the Owner shall acquire all rights to the commissioned Work including copyright.

The Author/Artist warrants that the Work will be original and will not infringe or plagiarize any other work; will not libel any person or invade any person's right to privacy; and, will not contain any unlawful materials. The Author/Artist shall indemnify and save the Owner harmless from any loss or liability due to any breach of these warranties, including reasonable attorney's fees.

The Author/Artist shall be responsible for all costs in creation of the Work unless otherwise agreed to in writing by the Owner.

This agreement shall be governed by the laws of __North Carolina__.

If any part of this agreement is adjudged invalid, illegal, or unenforceable, the remaining parts shall not be affected and shall remain in full force and effect.

This agreement shall be binding upon the parties, and upon their heirs, executors, personal representatives, administrators, and assigns. No person shall have a right or cause of action arising out of or resulting from this agreement except those who are parties to it and their successors in interest.

This instrument, including any attached exhibits and addenda, constitutes the entire agreement of the parties. No representations or promises have been made except those that are set out in this agreement. This agreement may not be modified except in writing signed by all the parties.

IN WITNESS WHEREOF the parties have signed this agreement under seal on ___7/10/08___.

Owner: Author/Artist:

_____   _____

_____   _____

Sample of Form 48: Assignment of Copyright

ASSIGNMENT OF COPYRIGHT

This Assignment is made this __12th__ day of __August__, __2008__, between __Arthur Author__ as Owner of the copyright on the Work known as _A History of Scrupulousness_, and _____Scrupulous Corporation_____ as Purchaser.

WHEREAS the Owner is sole owner of all rights in the Work and whereas the Purchaser is desirous of purchasing all such rights,

IT IS AGREED between the parties hereto that in consideration of the sum of $__14,650.00__, the receipt of which is hereby acknowledged, the Owner hereby assigns to the Purchaser all his/her interest in the Work and the copyright thereon, which interest shall be held for the full term of said copyright.

IN WITNESS WHEREOF, the Owner has executed this Agreement on the date above written.

_____

STATE OF North Carolina   )
COUNTY OF Scupernong   )

I certify that _____Arthur Author_____ ,who ☒ is personally known to me to be the person whose name is subscribed to the foregoing instrument ☐ produced _____ as identification, personally appeared before me on __Aug. 12, 2008__, and ☒ acknowledged the execution of the foregoing instrument ☐ acknowledged that (s)he is (Assistant) Secretary of _____and that by authority duly given and as the act of the corporation, the foregoing instrument was signed in its name by its (Vice) President, sealed with its corporate seal, and attested by him/her as its (Assistant) Secretary.

_____
Nan Notation
Notary Public, State of North Carolina
Notary's commission expires: 8/15/2010

Sample of Form 49: Copyright License

COPYRIGHT LICENSE

This License is made this __21st__ day of __February__, __2009__, between __Bonita Fides__ as Owner of the copyright on the Work known as __*Scruples Around the World*__ and __Scrupulous Corporation__ as Licensee.

WHEREAS the Owner is sole owner of all rights in the Work and whereas the Licensee is desirous of purchasing rights in said Work;

IT IS AGREED between the parties hereto that in consideration of the sum of $__7,500.00__, the receipt of which is hereby acknowledged, the Owner hereby licenses the License to use the copyrighted Work as follows:

It is understood between the parties that this License covers only those uses listed above for the time period stated. All other rights in and to the copyrighted work shall remain the property of the Owner.

This agreement shall be governed by the laws of __North Carolina__.

If any part of this agreement is adjudged invalid, illegal, or unenforceable, the remaining parts shall not be affected and shall remain in full force and effect.

This agreement shall be binding upon the parties, and upon their heirs, executors, personal representatives, administrators, and assigns. No person shall have a right or cause of action arising out of or resulting from this agreement except those who are parties to it and their successors in interest.

This instrument, including any attached exhibits and addenda, constitutes the entire agreement of the parties. No representations or promises have been made except those that are set out in this agreement. This agreement may not be modified except in writing signed by all the parties.

IN WITNESS WHEREOF the parties have signed this agreement under seal on __February 21, 2009__.

Owner: Licensee:

_____   _____

_____   _____

Indemnification   Employees may be reluctant to work in certain capacities (especially as corporate officers) if there is a danger they may get sued. It may help to offer the employee an **INDEMNIFICATION AGREEMENT**. (see form 62, p.261.) This is simply an agreement whereby the employer agrees to pay for any consequences of a lawsuit against the employee. Generally, state law requires corporations, limited partnerships, and limited liability companies to provide mandatory indemnification to officers and directors who are sued in that capacity and prevail in the lawsuit.

Sample of Form 62: Indemnification Agreement

INDEMNIFICATION AGREEMENT

In exchange for ___Permission to use the auditorium at 203 Songbird Avenue as___ ___described below___ and other valuable consideration, the receipt and sufficiency of which is hereby acknowledged, the undersigned hereby agrees to indemnify and hold ___Scrupulous___ ___Corporation___ (the "Company") harmless from any claim, action, liability, or suit arising out of or in any way connected with the following:

The use by the undersigned, her guests, associates, and licensees, of the auditorium in the Company's headquarters building located at 203 Songbird Avenue for voice recital purposes on July 5th, 2009.

In the event any claim reasonably believed by the Company to be subject to indemnification under this agreement is asserted against the Company, the Company will provide timely notice of such claim to the undersigned. The undersigned will thereafter, at its own expense, defend and protect the Company against such claim. Should the undersigned be unable or fail to so defend the Company, the Company shall have the right to defend or settle such claim, and the undersigned shall reimburse the Company for all settlements, judgments, fees, costs, expenses, and payments, including reasonable attorney's fees, incurred by the Company in connection with the discharge of such claim.

This agreement shall be governed by the laws of ___North Carolina___.

If any part of this agreement is adjudged invalid, illegal, or unenforceable, the remaining parts shall not be affected and shall remain in full force and effect.

This agreement shall be binding upon the parties, and upon their heirs, executors, personal representatives, administrators, and assigns. No person shall have a right or cause of action arising out of or resulting from this agreement except those who are parties to it and their successors in interest.

This instrument, including any attached exhibits and addenda, constitutes the entire agreement of the parties. No representations or promises have been made except those that are set out in this agreement. This agreement may not be modified except in writing signed by all the parties.

IN WITNESS WHEREOF the parties have signed this agreement under seal on ___6/28/2009___.

_____   _____
_____   _____

Non-Competition Agreements

You may want to be sure that an employee does not learn your business, then quit to open his or her own business and compete with you. A **NON-COMPETITION AGREEMENT** may provide some protection from competition of a former employee. (see form 12, p.143.) Such an agreement typically prohibits the employee from competing within a certain geographical area and for a certain period of time (provided the restrictions are reasonable). As a matter of public policy, courts usually interpret such agreements restrictively because they limit an employee's choices about earning a living.

Sample of Form 12: Non-Competition Agreement

NON-COMPETITION AGREEMENT

This agreement is made between ____Faith Workman____ (the "Employee") and Scrupulous Corporation ____ (the "Employer").

The Employee agrees to the terms of this agreement:

☒ contemporaneously with and as part of the terms of the Employment Agreement by which the Employee is being hired by the Employer, which Employment Agreement is incorporated by reference.

☐ in consideration of the Employee's continued employment by the Employer and additional consideration consisting of _____, which the Employee acknowledges is sufficient consideration paid by the Employer over and above the consideration due to the Employee pursuant to his or her usual terms of employment.

1. The Employee agrees that he or she will not compete, directly or indirectly, as a business owner, partner, corporation, employee, agent, or otherwise with the business of the Employer or any of the Employer's successors or assigns.

2. "Not compete," as used herein, shall mean that the Employee, directly or indirectly, as an owner, partner, officer, director, stockholder, employee, consultant, agent, or otherwise (except as a passive investment stockholder in a publicly owned corporation), shall not engage in any business or activity described as: __sale, design, or production of any product produced by Employer__ __during the period of Employee's employment by Employer__ .

3. This agreement shall apply to such business or activity within the following geographical area: __within 50 miles of the company's principal office in the state of North Carolina__ , and shall remain in full force and effect for a period of __12 months following the termination__ __of Employee's employment by Employer__ .

4. In the event of any breach of this agreement by the Employee, the Employer shall be entitled to injunctive relief without posting any bond, in addition to any other legal rights and remedies.

5. This agreement shall be governed by the laws of __North Carolina__ .

6. If any part of this agreement is adjudged invalid, illegal, or unenforceable, the remaining parts shall not be affected and shall remain in full force and effect, and any such time period and geographical limitations stated in this agreement shall be amended to allow enforcement to the nearest extent permitted by law.

7. This agreement shall be binding upon the parties, and upon their heirs, executors, personal representatives, administrators, and assigns. No person shall have a right or cause of action arising out of or resulting from this agreement except those who are parties to it and their successors in interest.

8. This instrument, including any attached exhibits and addenda, constitutes the entire agreement of the parties. No representations or promises have been made except those that are set out in this agreement. This agreement may not be modified except in writing signed by all the parties.

IN WITNESS WHEREOF the parties have signed this agreement under seal on 10/6/2009 .

Employer:

Employee:

_____

_____

_____

_____

REFERENCES

There was a time when employers treated references for former employees lightly. Glowing references were given routinely, and if they were less than glowing, so be it. No more. If a former employee's prospective new employer asks you for a reference, and you mislead him or her, you could conceivably be liable for damages to the new employer caused by hiring a bad employee.

Example:

You know your former employee had stolen from the company, but you do not mention it in a letter of recommendation. The employee later steals quite a lot from the new employer. Will you be liable for not mentioning the history of theft?

There may also be liability from the other direction.

Example:

Suppose you say something less than flattering about a former employee and it turns out to be untrue (or you just cannot prove it). Will you be liable for defamation?

Many employers now refuse to give references and will only confirm dates of employment and salary history. The following is a response to a request for references that provides only limited information.

Sample Response to Inquiry Regarding Former Employee

Scrupulous Corporation of America ————————————————————————————
400 West 61st Avenue, P.O. Box 19
New York, NY 10032

October 12, 2008

George Dempsey, Personnel Director
Kent, Goldsmith & Fargo, P.A.
2473 Washington St., Suite 2300
Philadelphia, PA 10607

Dear Mr. Dempsey:

We have received your request for a reference regarding a former employee of this company. It is our policy not to provide such references or disclose reasons for termination. However, we are able to confirm that Jean Walker was employed by us from March 1, 1997, through September 12, 2007. Her ending rate of pay was $22,000 per year.

No conclusion adverse to our former employee should be drawn from this response. Our policy with regard to references does not imply any dissatisfaction with the performance or conduct of any former employee.

Sincerely,

Carl Franklin

Carl Franklin,
Personnel Director

chapter 3

Independent Contractors

EMPLOYEE VERSUS INDEPENDENT CONTRACTOR

Whether someone is an *employee* or an *independent contractor* is an important distinction. An employer owes significant legal duties to an employee that it may not owe to an independent contractor. Perhaps even more importantly, an employer owes duties to the government on account of an employee such as taxes, workers' compensation, and the like. An employer may be liable to a third party for the negligence of an employee where it would not be liable for the negligence of an independent contractor.

And it is not always easy to tell which is which. Just because you and someone you hire explicitly agree between yourselves at the time of the hire that it will be an independent contractor relationship does not mean a court or the IRS will agree with you if the issue comes up later.

There is a list of factors to be considered. A "yes" answer to all or most of the following questions will likely mean that the person hired is an independent contractor rather than an employee (for more information and certainty, get IRS Form SS-8, available at the nearest IRS office or online at **www.irs.gov/pub/irs-pdf/fss8.pdf**).

   1. Does the person hired exercise independent control over the details of the work such as the methods used to complete the job?

2.   Is the person hired in a business different from that of the person hiring? (For example, where a plumber is hired by a lawyer.)

3.   Does the person hired work as a specialist without supervision by the person hiring?

4.   Does the person hired supply his or her own tools?

5.   Is the person hired for only a short period of time rather than consistently over a relatively long period?

6.   Does the job require a relatively high degree of skill?

7.   Is the person paid by the job rather than by the hour?

Independent Contractors

Contracts with independent contractors do not usually have to be in writing, but it is often even more important that they are written than having an employment agreement be in writing. For one thing, the writing is an opportunity to state clearly that you intend it to be an independent contractor arrangement. Also, since by definition you have relatively little control over the way an independent contractor does the work, the writing may be your last chance to influence important matters like exactly what the job is and when it must be completed.

It is often tempting to use the word *employer* in these contracts; however, it is not appropriate since the independent contractor is not an employee (and you do not want the IRS thinking otherwise). The samples on pages 43–45 are two examples of independent contractor contracts.

Sample of Form 13: Appointment of Independent Sales Representative (Payment by Commission)

APPOINTMENT OF INDEPENDENT SALES REPRESENTATIVE

This agreement is entered into by and between _____Howard Parsons_____ (the "Agent") and _____Scrupulous Corporation_____ (the "Company"). It is agreed by the Agent and the Company as follows:

1.   The Company has appointed the Agent as its representative for the sale of __products__ in the following territory: __Alabama, Florida, Georgia, and Mississippi__. The territory may be changed from time to time upon agreement by the Company and the Agent. The Agent agrees to use his or her best efforts in the sale of such in the territory assigned.

2.   The term of Agent's appointment shall begin on _____January 1, 2009_____, and may be ended by the Agent or by the Company at any time and for any reason.

3.   All sales made by the Agent shall be at prices and terms set by the Company, and no sales contracts shall be valid until accepted by a duly authorized officer of the Company.

4.   The Agent's compensation and benefits during the term of this agreement shall be as stated in this paragraph, and may be adjusted from time to time by the Company. The Company shall pay the Agent a commission of _____10__% based on the net selling price of the goods actually received by the Company. In the event part or all of the purchase price is refunded to the purchaser for any reason, the Agent's commission based on such amounts refunded shall be returned by the Agent to the Company or deducted by the Company from the Agent's future commissions. The Company shall not be liable to the Agent for commissions on orders unfilled by the Company for any reason. In addition to the commissions provided for in this agreement, the Agent shall receive _____$100/wk. expense account__.

5.   The Company shall reimburse the Agent for expenses according to a schedule published from time to time by the Company.

6.   The parties agree that no employer-employee relationship is created by this agreement, but the relationship of the Agent to the Company shall be that of an independent contractor.

7.   This agreement shall be governed by the laws of _____Florida_____. If any part of this agreement is adjudged invalid, illegal, or unenforceable, the remaining parts shall not be affected and shall remain in full force and effect. This agreement shall be binding upon the parties, and upon their heirs, executors, personal representatives, administrators, and assigns. No person shall have a right or cause of action arising out of or resulting from this agreement except those who are parties to it and their successors in interest.

8.   This instrument, including any attached exhibits and addenda, constitutes the entire agreement of the parties. No representations or promises have been made except those that are set out in this agreement. This agreement may not be modified except in writing signed by all the parties.

IN WITNESS WHEREOF the parties have signed this agreement under seal on _____December 22, 2008_____.

Company: Agent:

_____Scrupulous Corporation_____   _____*Howard Parsons*_____

_____   _____

Sample of Form 15: Independent Contractor Agreement

INDEPENDENT CONTRACTOR AGREEMENT

This agreement is entered into by and between ___Stainproof Carpets, Inc.___ (the "Company") and _____Joe King_____ (the "Contractor"). It is agreed by the parties as follows:

1.   The Contractor shall supply all the labor and materials to perform the following work for the Company as an independent contractor:

Installation of carpet and pad in five residences listed in paragraph 2 below; carpet and pad to be provided by the Company.

❏ The attached plans and specifications are to be followed and are hereby made a part of this Agreement.

2.   The Contractor agrees to the following completion dates for portions of the work and final completion of the work:

Description of Work	Completion Date
1492 Columbus Dr.	October 4, 2008
1776 S. Washington Blvd.	October 5, 2008
1066 Normandy Lane	October 6, 2008
1929 Wall Street	October 7, 2008
1215 Magna Carta Cir.	October 9, 2008

3.   The Contractor shall perform the work in a workmanlike manner, according to standard industry practices, unless other standards or requirements are set forth in any attached plans and specifications.

4.   The Company shall pay the Contractor the sum of $___$1,750.00___, in full payment for the work as set forth in this Agreement, to be paid as follows:

5.   Any additional work or services shall be agreed to in writing, signed by both parties.

6.   The Contractor shall obtain and maintain any licenses or permits necessary for the work to be performed. The Contractor shall obtain and maintain any required insurance, including but not limited to workers' compensation insurance, to cover the Contractor's employees and agents.

7.   The Contractor shall be responsible for the payment of any sub-contractors and shall obtain lien releases from sub-contractors as may be necessary. The Contractor agrees to indemnify and hold harmless the Company from any claims or liability arising out of the work performed by the Contractor under this Agreement.

8.   Time is of the essence of this Agreement.

9.   This instrument, including any attached exhibits and addenda, constitutes the entire agreement of the parties. No representations or promises have been made except those that are set

out in this agreement. This agreement may not be modified except in writing signed by all the parties.

10. This agreement shall be governed by the laws of _____North Carolina_____.

IN WITNESS WHEREOF the parties have signed this agreement under seal on _____September 30, 2008_____.

Company: Stainproof Carpet, Inc.

George T. Berber
_____
George T. Berber, President

Attest:___*Margaret G. Saxony*___
Margaret G. Saxony, Secretary

(Corporate Seal)

Contractor: Joe King

___*Joe King*_____(Seal)
Joe King

CONSULTANTS

Consultants are a category of independent contractors. Frequently they are hired without any sort of written agreement, but it is hard to imagine a situation in which a written agreement is not better. Many consultants will have their own standard form agreements for you to sign.

Accountants

Accountants provide a variety of services, from bookkeeping and the preparation of tax forms to the formal audit of a company's financial statements. Audits are expensive and, for most corporations, not necessary. An audit may be required by some regulatory agency or by contract with some institution. Be careful that you do not lightly sign an agreement with a lender or some other party that requires the production of *audited financial statements*. You may be getting into more than you bargained for.

Lawyers

Lawyers are predictably creative about the ways in which you can pay them. Usually contracts for legal services provide for payment by the hour, by the task, or, where the client is a plaintiff in a lawsuit asking for money damages, on a contingent basis. A *contingent fee* is an arrangement in which the lawyer gets a share of the client's recovery. Always insist on a written fee agreement with a lawyer.

Powers of Attorney

A *power of attorney* is a written authority for someone to act as your agent. The agent is often called an *attorney in fact*. (This has no relationship to an *attorney at law,* except that a lawyer is an agent for legal matters.) Corporations do not ordinarily execute powers of attorney, because corporate officers are already the appointed agents of the company. If you want the vice president to perform some task on behalf of the company, you can simply have the board of directors authorize the act in a resolution. However, on some occasions it may be appropriate to use a power of attorney to authorize an officer, director, employee, or other person to perform a certain act.

A power of attorney can be for a particular duty and expire when that duty is done with a **LIMITED POWER OF ATTORNEY** (see form 17, p.155), or it can authorize a wide range of activity and last for an indefinite period of time with a general **POWER OF ATTORNEY**. (see form 18, p.157.) A power of attorney can usually be revoked at any time by the person giving it (who is called the *grantor*). Ordinarily, powers of attorney may be canceled at any time by the grantor. The sample of form 19, **REVOCATION OF POWER OF ATTORNEY**, on page 49 is a form for that purpose. Of course, the attorney in fact may resign an appointment at any time. The blank form is in the appendix. (see form 19, p.159.)

If the grantor were a corporation, the power of attorney would be signed by the president or vice president and attested by the secretary or assistant secretary. The notary would then notarize the secretary's signature. (See Chapter 1 for more information about signatures and notary acknowledgments.)

Sample of Form 17: Simple Power of Attorney for a Particular Purpose

---

LIMITED POWER OF ATTORNEY

      Scrupulous Enterprises   (the "Grantor") hereby grants
to   Roberta Moore   (the "Agent") a limited power of attorney.
As the Grantor's attorney in fact, the Agent shall have full power and authority to undertake and
perform the following on behalf of the Grantor: Execute a contract and financing documents for
the purchase and financing of a 2005 Chevrolet Astro delivery van.

      By accepting this grant, the Agent agrees to act in a fiduciary capacity consistent with the
reasonable best interests of the Grantor. This power of attorney may be revoked by the Grantor at
any time; however, any person dealing with the Agent as attorney in fact may rely on this appointment until receipt of actual notice of termination.

      IN WITNESS WHEREOF, the undersigned grantor has executed this power of attorney
under seal as of the ____10th____ day of _____May_____, ___2008___.

Scrupulous Enterprises,
a general partnership

Witness/Attest:____(Not applicable)____   *Henry Hardy* _____(Seal)
                Secretary   Grantor

STATE OF   NEW YORK
COUNTY OF JAMAICA

      I certify that _____Henry Hardy_____, who ☒ is personally known to me to be the
person whose name is subscribed to the foregoing instrument ❑ produced _____ as
identification, personally appeared before me on ___May 10, 2008_____, and ☒ acknowledged
the execution of the foregoing instrument ❑ acknowledged that (s)he is (Assistant) Secretary of
_____ and that by authority duly given and as the act of the corporation, the
foregoing instrument was signed in its name by its (Vice) President, sealed with its corporate seal,
and attested by him/her as its Secretary.

Calvin Collier
Notary Public, State of New York
Notary's commission expires: Oct. 31, 2010

      I hereby accept the foregoing appointment as attorney in fact on   May 10, 2008 .

Roberta Moore
Attorney in Fact

Sample of Form 18: Power of Attorney

POWER OF ATTORNEY

____Henry Hardy____ (the "Grantor") hereby grants to _____Roberta Moore_____ (the "Agent") a general power of attorney. As the Grantor's attorney in fact, the Agent shall have full power and authority to undertake any and all acts that may be lawfully undertaken on behalf of the grantor including, but not limited to, the right to buy, sell, lease, mortgage, assign, rent, or otherwise dispose of any real or personal property belonging to the Grantor; to execute, accept, undertake, and perform contracts in the name of the Grantor; to deposit, endorse, or withdraw funds to or from any bank depository of the Grantor; to initiate, defend, or settle legal actions on behalf of the Grantor; and to retain any accountant, attorney, or other advisor deemed by the Agent to be necessary to protect the interests of the Grantor in relation to such powers.

By accepting this grant, the Agent agrees to act in a fiduciary capacity consistent with the reasonable best interests of the Grantor. This power of attorney may be revoked by the Grantor at any time; however, any person dealing with the Agent as attorney in fact may rely on this appointment until receipt of actual notice of termination.

IN WITNESS WHEREOF, the undersigned grantor has executed this power of attorney under seal as of the __10th__ day of __March__, __2009__.

Witness/Attest:_____   _____(Seal)
Grantor

STATE OF New York
COUNTY OF Jamaica

I certify that _____Henry Hardy_____, who ☐ is personally known to me to be the person whose name is subscribed to the foregoing instrument ☒ produced ____U.S. Passport____ as identification, personally appeared before me on _____3/10/2009_____, and ☒ acknowledged the execution of the foregoing instrument ☒ acknowledged that (s)he is (Assistant) Secretary of _____ and that by authority duly given and as the act of the corporation, the foregoing instrument was signed in its name by its (Vice) President, sealed with its corporate seal, and attested by him/her as its (Assistant) Secretary.

_____Nathan Notary_____
Notary Public, State of New York
Notary's commission expires: 5/28/2011

I hereby accept the foregoing appointment as attorney in fact on _____3/10/2009_____.

_____Roberta Moore____ Attorney in Fact

Sample of Form 19: Revocation of Power of Attorney

REVOCATION OF POWER OF ATTORNEY

_____Henry Hardy_____ (the "Grantor") hereby revokes the Power of Attorney dated _____May 10, 2008_____, appointing _____James Bond_____ as the Agent and attorney in fact to act on behalf of the Grantor.

This revocation shall be effective on the _1st_ day of ___June___, 20 _08_ .

_____*Henry Hardy*_____ (Signature of Grantor)

_____Henry Hardy_____ (Typed or printed name of Grantor)

I hereby acknowledge receipt of the foregoing revocation of power of attorney on the _1st_ day of __June__, 20 _08_ .

_____*James Bond*_____

Attorney in Fact

Buying, Selling, and Leasing Real Estate

chapter 5

BUYING AND SELLING REAL ESTATE

Unless you are in the business of purchasing, developing, and reselling real property, it is likely that the decision to buy or sell land or buildings represents a significant step. It will follow careful and possibly quite lengthy consideration, including a period of investigation, appraisal, and thought about the future of your business. If your business is a corporation or some form of partnership, the issue may be visited several times by the board of directors or partners who may want to be involved at every step.

Buying and selling real estate has been going on for thousands of years. One of the reasons we human beings developed law in the first place was to protect the ownership of real estate without the need for armed combat. So the laws are old and, like the lands they deal with, they are uniquely tied to and vary with the jurisdiction. Therefore, this chapter will explain certain matters to be considered in dealing with real estate and the type of forms commonly used, but it will not contain many forms you can use.

If you are purchasing or selling commercial real estate, you should consult a real estate attorney. A lawyer who knows the applicable state law and even the recording customs at the local court house will be indispensable even for small real estate transactions. He or she will know what to do about title searches, insurance, and countless little details that will loom large if not handled correctly. A real estate purchase is a major step for your business, one that is too important to venture into without professional advice. That said, we will now discuss some of the more common forms you will encounter.

Real estate forms specific for your state can usually be obtained from a real estate sales office (for sales contracts and options) or an office supply store (for deeds).

Options to Purchase

An *option* is a kind of contract within a contract. It is an agreement to keep an offer open for a period of time in exchange for some consideration such as money. As always in a contract, the consideration part is important. It must be real and not just a formal recital or else you might find that you do not have an option at all. Options may be recorded in the same way deeds are. Recording will protect the party with the option from subsequent claims, but it may also trigger a due on sale clause in an existing mortgage.

Contract for Purchase and Sale

A *contract for purchase and sale* is usually the first formal step toward a purchase. It is a formal contract that spells out the terms under which the seller agrees to sell and the buyer agrees to buy. Typically such a contract will be elaborate, especially if, for example, it concerns a complex structure occupied by existing tenants and subject to existing mortgages.

It would be unwise to attempt to provide a usable contract for purchase and sale of real estate in this book, when entire books are devoted to this single type of document.

Deeds

A *deed* is a document that formally transfers title, or ownership, of property. There are several types of deeds in regular use. In most cases, you probably need a *warranty deed* in which the seller guarantees, among other things, that he or she has good title to the property, and that after selling it the buyer will have good title.

What makes a warranty deed special is language such as the following [*explanatory notes are in brackets*]:

To have and to hold such property together with all rights and appurtenances thereto belonging [*the buyer will be granted the property and everything that goes with it*]. The grantor is seized of the premises in fee simple [*the seller owns the property outright*] and has the right to convey the same in fee simple [*has the right to transfer the property free and clear*], and the grantor hereby covenants to warrant and forever defend title to the property against the lawful claims of all persons whomsoever except for the exceptions stated above. [*The seller promises that if anyone claims the buyer does not have good title, the seller will go to court to protect the buyer's ownership except for matters noted elsewhere. (For example, the existence of an outstanding mortgage would be noted elsewhere in the deed.)*]

An alternative deed, and the type you would prefer to use if you are the seller, is the *quitclaim deed*, which merely says that the seller sells to the buyer whatever the seller owns, if anything, with no guarantees. Quitclaim deeds have their uses, but you probably would not buy property relying on a quitclaim deed alone, and it is unlikely that a knowledgeable person would accept one from you. These days most deeds are fill-in-the-blank forms, each state has its own preferred format, and some states have required formats.

Transfers of real property are usually made under seal and acknowledged. They are within the Statute of Frauds and must be in writing (see Chapter 1). Since real property cannot be literally handed over to the buyer, recording of deeds is critical. It is the way you prove your ownership and the way you prevent someone else from purporting to sell the property that belongs to you.

Sample Typical Warranty Deed

State of North Carolina

Elon County

THIS DEED, made this 28th day of June, 2008, by SCRUPULOUS CORPORATION, Grantor, to THE PARTICULAR PARTNERSHIP, Grantee, of Elon County, North Carolina:

Witnesseth: That the Grantor, in consideration of Ten Dollars and other valuable consideration to them paid by the Grantee, the receipt of which is hereby acknowledged, has bargained and sold, and by these presents do grant, bargain, sell, and convey unto the Grantee, their heirs, or successors, and assigns, the parcel of land in Elon County, North Carolina, in Croatan Township, more particularly described as follows:

LOT 4, BLOCK 3 OF THE CROATAN INDUSTRIAL PARK ACCORDING TO A MAP THEREOF RECORDED IN MAP BOOK 1911 AT PAGE 9, ELON COUNTY REGISTRY.

This property was conveyed to the Grantor by deed dated July 10, 1996, recorded in Book 2307 Page 1239 Elon County Registry.

TO HAVE AND TO HOLD the aforesaid parcel of land and all privileges and appurtenances thereunto belonging to the said Grantee, its heirs, or successors, and assigns forever.

And the said Scrupulous Corporation for itself and its successors covenants with the Grantee, its heirs, successors, and assigns that it is seized of the said premises in fee and the right to convey the same in fee simple; that the same are free from encumbrances except as herein set forth; and that it will warrant and defend the said title to the same against the claims of all persons whomsoever.

The plural number as used herein shall equally include the singular. The masculine or feminine gender as used herein shall equally include the neuter.

This deed is signed by the corporation under seal by authority of its board of directors on the day and year first above written.

Scrupulous Corporation

By: _Henry Hardy_____

Henry Hardy, President

(Corporate Seal)   Attest: _Calvin Collier_____

Calvin Collier, Secretary

State of North Carolina

Elon County

I certify that ___Calvin Collier___ personally appeared before me on June 28th, 2008, and acknowledged that he is Secretary of ___Scrupulous Corporation___ and that by authority duly given and as the act of the corporation, the foregoing instrument was signed in its name by its President, sealed with its corporate seal, and attested by him as its Secretary.

_____

Notary Public, State of North Carolina

My Commission Expires: Sept. 30, 2010

Signatures

As always, the signatures on options, contracts for purchase and sale, and deeds must be appropriate for the situation, depending upon whether the property owner is an individual, married couple, partnership, corporation, etc. (See the section on "Signatures" in Chapter 1.)

Closing the Sale

A real estate closing can be a monumental paper shuffle, especially if the property is complex commercial property. Once again, the value of an attorney experienced in the procedure will be indispensable. But you have a part, too. Keep an eye on the details. Before the closing, become as familiar as you can with the documents that will pass under your nose. You will know what is important to you better than your lawyer will. There will not be much time for reading and explanations at the closing, and what time there is will likely be charged to you by the hour.

Securing Payment

Real estate is commonly used to secure payment of a debt, either in connection with the purchase of real property or to secure a loan unconnected with a real estate purchase. This is done with a *mortgage*, although some states use a document called a *deed of trust*. A mortgage or deed of trust will describe the real estate, refer to the promissory note it secures, and have numerous provisions relating to what happens if the promissory note goes into default. If your property is being mortgaged, the lender on the promissory note will probably prepare the mortgage documents.

If you are going to take a mortgage to secure money someone owes to you, you will need to prepare the documents. Since the form for a mortgage, and the requirements for its execution and recording, vary from state to state, no useful form can be provided in a book like this. Mortgage forms can usually be obtained from an office supply store, or possibly from a real estate agent, bank, or mortgage company. If you hold a mortgage, you may want to sell it to another party. To do so, you will need to execute an **ASSIGNMENT OF MORTGAGE**. (see form 23, p.167.) If you hold the mortgage until it is paid off, you will need to execute a **SATISFACTION OF MORTGAGE**. (see form 24, p.169.)

LEASING REAL ESTATE

Leasing real property is a lot like buying it. In fact, you are buying it for a period of time, so the process is in some ways similar. A lease or rental agreement is the document that affects the right to temporary possession of real estate. Although it transfers an interest in real estate, as does a deed, a lease is a very different animal. Deeds are usually quite short. Leases are usually quite long. Deeds look very much alike, while leases vary tremendously depending upon the type and function of the property being leased. Residential leases are different from commercial leases.

Some states have required clauses, relating to such matters as security deposits, lead-based paints, and radon testing. The failure to include one of these required clauses could render the lease unenforceable or create some kind of penalty for the landlord. As with buying and selling real estate, you should consult a real estate attorney before signing a lease. Especially in a long-term commercial lease, or one with renewal options, a lot of money can be at stake.

The **RESIDENTIAL LEASE AGREEMENT** and the **COMMERCIAL LEASE AGREEMENT** are among the forms at the back of this book. They are typical examples of leases. (see form 40, p.201 and form 41, p.211.)

MANAGING THE LEASE

Unlike the sale and purchase of real estate where, after the closing, there is ordinarily little reason for the buyer to be in contact with the seller, a lease is an ongoing relationship. It may require attention or changing from time to time. It may have to be terminated. The following are documents designed to take care of some of the problems that may come up.

Amendments

Amendments to a lease come in many forms. Sometimes they are called *riders* or *addenda*. Whatever the name, the purpose is to make a change in the standard terms of a lease or terms that have already been agreed upon. Before you sign an amendment, read the provision of the basic lease that says how and under what conditions the lease may be amended. Make sure the amendment you sign conforms to those conditions.

Sample of Form 44: Amendment to Real Property Lease Agreement

AMENDMENT TO REAL PROPERTY LEASE AGREEMENT

For valuable consideration, the receipt and sufficiency of which is hereby acknowledged by each of the parties, this agreement amends a lease agreement (the "Lease") between __Stripmall Rentals, Inc.__ (the "Landlord") and __Scrupulous Associates, a general partnership__ (the "Tenant") dated__ September 7, 2008 __, relating to property located at ___16249 W. 24th_____ ___Street, Unit 6, Austin, Texas_____. This agreement is hereby incorporated into the Lease.

1. Paragraph 5 of the Lease is hereby amended to read in its entirety as follows:

   5. Assignment. The Tenant shall not assign this Agreement or sublet the Premises in whole or in part without the written consent of the Landlord.

2. Paragraph 20.3 of the Lease is hereby deleted in its entirety.

3. There is hereby added to the Lease a new paragraph number 9.4, which shall read in its entirety as follows:

   9.4. Provide the Tenant with 10 designated and sign-posted parking spaces in the center parking lot.

Except as changed by this amendment, the Lease shall continue in effect according to its terms. The amendments herein shall be effective on the date this document is executed by both parties.

Executed on ____ September 7, 2008 ___.

Landlord: StripMall Rentals, Inc.   Tenant: Scrupulous Associates

_____*Albert Smith*_____   _____*Henry Hardy*_____(Seal)
Albert Smith, President   Henry Hardy, General Partner

Assignments and Sublets

Chapter 1 discussed the assignment of contracts. From the tenant's point of view, assigning a lease means moving out and finding a new tenant. When a landlord assigns a lease, it is usually called *assigning rents*.

Assignments and sublets are different. In an *assignment*, the new tenant steps into the shoes of the old tenant and deals with the landlord directly. If all goes well, the old tenant is out of the picture. Remember that while a tenant can assign his or her right to use the property, he or she can only delegate the duty to pay rent. This means that, absent an agreement by the landlord, the tenant always remains ultimately responsible for payment of the rent if the lease assignee fails to do so. (The **LEASE ASSIGNMENT** sample of form 42 on page 60–61 provides an optional provision in which the landlord discharges the old tenant from further obligations under the lease. In the example, the partnership tenant has incorporated, and the lease is being assigned to the corporation.)

In a *sublease*, the old tenant stands between the landlord and the subtenant. In essence, the tenant becomes landlord to the subtenant. The subtenant will pay rent to the old tenant, who will then pay rent to the landlord. The subtenant may pay more rent to the tenant than the tenant will pay to the landlord, leaving the tenant a profit. A sublease is actually a special type of lease and is just as complex as a lease. The failure to include certain provisions required by a state or local law can invalidate a sublease; therefore, you should consult an attorney or a book specifically about leases before preparing or signing one. Because of the variety of state and local leasing laws, it is not practical to provide a sublease form in this book.

Almost every written lease agreement will require the landlord's permission before the tenant can validly assign the lease or sublet the premises. (see form 39, p.199; form 40, p.201; and form 41, p.211.) Examples of a **LEASE ASSIGNMENT** and a **LANDLORD'S CONSENT TO SUBLEASE** follow. The sample of form 42 makes the landlord a party giving consent to an assignment. As stated earlier, an assignment may or may not release the original tenant from further liability to the landlord, so be sure to note the language of each option within paragraph 4 in the example.

Sample of Form 42: Lease Assignment

LEASE ASSIGNMENT

This Lease Assignment is entered into by and among _____ Scrupulous Associates _____ (the "Assignor"), __ Scrupulous Corporation __ (the "Assignee"), and __ Peachtree Properties, Inc. __ (the "Landlord"). For valuable consideration, it is agreed by the parties as follows:

1. The Landlord and the Assignor have entered into a lease agreement (the "Lease") dated _____ April 1, 2008 _____, concerning the premises described as:

1264 Main Street, #24, Decatur, Georgia.

2. The Assignor hereby assigns and transfers to the Assignee all of Assignor's rights and delegates all of Assignor's duties under the Lease effective _____ October 1, 2008 _____ (the "Effective Date").

3. The Assignee hereby accepts such assignment of rights and delegation of duties and agrees to pay all rents promptly when due and perform all of Assignor's obligations under the Lease accruing on and after the Effective Date. The Assignee further agrees to indemnify and hold the Assignor harmless from any breach of Assignee's duties hereunder.

4. ❏ The Assignor agrees to transfer possession of the leased premises to the Assignee on the Effective Date. All rents and obligations of the Assignor under the Lease accruing before the Effective Date shall have been paid or discharged.

   ☒ The Landlord hereby assents to the assignment of the Lease hereunder and as of the Effective Date hereby releases and discharges the Assignor from all duties and obligations under the Lease accruing after the Effective Date.

   ❏ The Landlord hereby assents to assignment of this lease provided that Landlord's assent shall not discharge the Assignor of any obligations under the Lease in the event of breach by the Assignee. The Landlord will give notice to the Assignor of any breach by the Assignee. If the Assignor pays all accrued rents and cures any other default of the Assignee, the Assignor may enforce the terms of the Lease and this Assignment against the Assignee, in the name of the Landlord, if necessary.

5. There shall be no further assignment of the Lease without the written consent of the Landlord.

6. This agreement shall be binding upon and inure to the benefit of the parties, their successors, assigns, and personal representatives.

This assignment was executed under seal on _____ September 27, 2008 _____.

Assignor: Scrupulous Associates,
a general partnership

By___*Henry Hardy*___
Henry Hardy, General Partner

_____

Landlord: Peachtree Properties, Inc.

By___*Leigh Jackson*___
Leigh Jackson, President

Attest: ___*Susan Murphy*___
Susan Murphy, Secretary

Assignee: Scrupulous Corporation

By___*Henry Hardy*___
Henry Hardy, President

Attest: ___*Calvin Collier*___
Calvin Collier, Secretary

Sample of Form 45: Landlord's Consent to Sublease

LANDLORD'S CONSENT TO SUBLEASE

FOR VALUABLE CONSIDERATION, the undersigned (the "Landlord") hereby consents to the sublease of all or part of the premises located at __1264 Main Street, #24, Decatur, Georgia__, which is the subject of a lease agreement between Landlord and __Scrupulous Associates__ (the "Tenant"), pursuant to an Agreement to Sublease dated __April 1, 2008__, between the Tenant and __Scrupulous Corporation__ as Subtenant dated __September 26, 2008__.

This consent was signed by the Landlord on __September 28, 2008__.

Landlord: Peachtree Properties, Inc.

By: ___*Leigh Jackson*___
Leigh Jackson, President

Landlord's assignment. As often as not, it is the landlord, not the tenant, who assigns a lease. For example, suppose the landlord sells the rented property. The new owner of the property will also be the new owner of the lease. The tenant will thereafter owe the rent to the new landlord and look to the new owner (in legal terms, will *attorn* to the new owner) to repair the plumbing and otherwise take over the role of landlord.

Before the new owner buys the property, he or she will need assurance that any leases being purchased are valid and not in default. The seller of the property, the old landlord, will provide some of these assurances, but the new owner will need more. He or she will want the tenant to sign a letter, called an *estoppel letter*, acknowledging that the tenant recognizes the terms of the lease, has kept the rent up to date, and does not consider the landlord's obligations under the lease to be in default. Signing such a letter prevents the tenant from later contradicting the estoppel letter (*estop* means *prevent* or *impede*) by claiming that the terms of the lease are different from the new owner's understanding, or that the lease was in default when the assignment took place. The **ESTOPPEL LETTER** is typical of such a letter. (see form 43, p.223.)

Extending or Renewing a Lease

Almost any lease will have a provision stating the terms under which it may be extended or renewed. Sometimes advance notice of intent to renew (or to not renew) is required. It is important to read such provisions and comply with them exactly.

Sample Notice of Intent to Renew or Extend Lease

Scrupulous Corporation of America ——————————————————

201 Wacker Drive, Suite 622
Chicago, IL 60602

November 23, 2008

201 Wacker Drive, Inc.
201 Wacker Drive, Suite 1012
Chicago, IL 60602

Dear Sir or Madam:

Pursuant to paragraph (3) of the Lease Agreement between you as Landlord and the undersigned as Tenant dated December 23, 1999, related to the premises located at 201 Wacker Drive, Suite 622, notice is hereby given of our intent to renew such lease for an additional term of two years.

Very truly yours,

Henry Hardy

Terminating a Lease

Here we are discussing the termination of a lease at the end of some appropriate term—not termination in mid-term for violation of the terms of the lease. Some leases provide for the termination of the lease upon the occurrence of some event or the passage of a certain amount of time. Some leases operate on a month-to-month basis and continue in effect until notice of termination is given by the landlord or tenant.

Either the lease or state law may require a written notice of termination. Failure to give written notice within a required time frame may result in automatic renewal of the lease. Again, it is important to read your lease and comply exactly with whatever termination provisions it contains, and to know your state's landlord/tenant laws. These laws may also be different for residential and commercial leases. Below is an example of a termination notice given by the tenant, but a slight rearrangement of the words would make it work for a landlord giving notice to a tenant.

Sample Notice of Termination of Lease

Scrupulous Corporation
201 Wacker Drive, Suite 622
Chicago, IL 60602

November 23, 2008

201 Wacker Drive, Inc.
201 Wacker Drive, Suite 1012
Chicago, IL 60602

Dear Sir or Madam:

Pursuant to paragraph (6) of the Lease Agreement between you as Landlord and the undersigned as Tenant dated December 23, 2007, related to the premises located at 201 Wacker Drive, Suite 622, notice is hereby given that such lease agreement is terminated effective December 31, 2008.

Very truly yours,

Henry Hardy

Agreement to Cancel

Occasionally the landlord and tenant, for whatever reason, will decide to call it quits. Leases, like any contract, can be terminated upon the mutual agreement of the parties. The following sample is a mutual agreement to terminate an existing lease. (Also see "Terminating Contracts" in Chapter 1.)

Sample of Form 47: Agreement to Cancel Lease

AGREEMENT TO CANCEL LEASE

The undersigned have entered into a lease agreement dated December 23, 2007, related to the premises known as 201 Wacker Drive, Suite 622 (the "Lease"). The undersigned acknowledge that, for valuable consideration and by their mutual agreement, effective on November 30, 2008, such Lease is hereby terminated and all rights and obligations of either party shall be canceled except for any obligations under the Lease accrued before the effective termination date.

This termination agreement shall be binding upon the parties, their successors, assigns, and personal representatives.

This termination agreement was signed on November 23, 2008.

Landlord: 201 Wacker Drive, Inc.   Tenant: Scrupulous Corporation

By___*Robert Johnson*_____   By _____*Henry Hardy*_____
Robert Johnson, President   Henry Hardy, President

Attest:__*William R. Smith*_____   Attest:____*Calvin Collier*_____
William R. Smith, Secretary   Calvin Collier, Secretary
(Corporate Seal)   (Corporate Seal)

Lease Compliance

Both parties to a lease have a variety of duties. The tenant mostly is required to pay money from time to time, but may also have repair and maintenance duties. The landlord will have some repair duties as well. The following form is an example of the main body of a demand letter. **Renter's Demand for Action by Landlord** is another form demanding compliance with lease terms. (see form 46, p.229.)

Sample of Demand for Compliance with Lease Terms

Dear Sir or Madam:

We call your attention to paragraph (7) of the Lease Agreement between you as Landlord and the undersigned as Tenant, dated December 23, 2007, related to the premises located at 201 Wacker Drive, Suite 622. Pursuant to that paragraph, you are required to provide weekly office cleaning services.

As of the date of this letter, you have failed to perform as required in that no office cleaning services have been provided for the past four weeks. We hereby demand that you comply with such provision immediately.

Buying, Selling, and Renting Merchandise and Equipment

This chapter is written mostly for the benefit of the business that occasionally purchases, sells, or leases equipment, incidental to its regular business. The implications of selling and leasing equipment *as a business* are beyond the scope of this book. If you are in the business of selling or leasing equipment, you should do extra research to develop a comprehensive set of forms specific to your needs. As a practical matter, if you are purchasing from a dealer, the seller will usually have its own forms. Similarly, if you are renting equipment from someone in the business of renting equipment, the lessor will usually have its own forms.

However, you may find that you want to purchase, sell, rent from, or rent to a friend, business acquaintance, family member, or business partner. For example, your tax advisor may suggest that, instead of having your business purchase a new computer, you would be better off buying a computer yourself and then leasing it to your company. (Perhaps this would allow your business more of a deduction for equipment rental payments than it would get from depreciating a computer the business owned.) Whatever the reason, this chapter will help you with such occasional purchases, sales, and leases.

SALE OR PURCHASE OF EQUIPMENT ON AN INSTALLMENT PLAN

Installment Sale Documents

A simple cash purchase will usually just involve a **BILL OF SALE**, as in the sample on page 71. (see form 29, p.179.) Several forms may be used in an installment sale. There may be a **SALES AGREEMENT** like the sample on page 69. (see form 27, p.175.) Often there are at least two other separate contracts used to complete an installment sale: a **SECURITY AGREEMENT** (sample of form 25 is on page 70), and a **PROMISSORY NOTE** (samples of form 22 are in Chapter 8). If these are combined into one document, it keeps the note part from being negotiable.

If the seller keeps a lien on the equipment as protection should the buyer fail to pay, then a Uniform Commercial Code financing statement (UCC-1) will be needed (see Chapter 8). If the equipment is a motor vehicle or boat, there will be a different system for recording security liens. Prior to the sale, you may want to have the buyer complete a **CREDIT APPLICATION**. (see form 20, p.161.)

Sample of Form 27: Sales Agreement

SALES AGREEMENT

This agreement is made by and between ____Scrupulous Corporation____ (the "Seller") and _____FBN, Inc._____ (the Buyer), who agree as follows:

1. The Seller agrees to sell, and the Buyer agrees to buy:

> Scrupulous Model S-250 stamping machine,
> serial number S-97-20938547

2. In exchange for the Property, the Buyer agrees to pay to the Seller the sum of $____30,000.00____, payable according to the terms of a promissory note, a copy of which is attached to this agreement and incorporated into this agreement by reference (the "Note").

3. The Seller retains a security interest in the Property to secure payment and performance of the Buyer's obligations under this agreement and the Note. Upon any default by the Buyer in the performance of any such obligations, the Seller may declare all obligations immediately due and payable and shall have the remedies of a secured party under the Uniform Commercial Code enacted in the state the laws of which govern the terms of this agreement.

This agreement is executed by the parties under seal on ____June 6____, _2008_.

Seller: Buyer:

Scrupulous Corporation   FBN, Inc.

_____*Henry Hardy*_____   _____*Marcia Bender*_____
Henry Hardy, President   Marcia Bender, President

_____*Calvin Collier*_____   _____*Matthew G. Bender*_____
Calvin Collier, Secretary   Matthew G. Bender, Secretary
(Corporate Seal)   (Corporate Seal)

Sample of Form 25: Security Agreement

SECURITY AGREEMENT

In exchange for valuable consideration, the receipt and sufficiency of which is hereby acknowledged by the undersigned, _____FBN, Inc._____ (the "Debtor") hereby grants to _____Scrupulous Corporation_____ (the "Creditor") a security interest in __Scrupulous Model S-250 stamping machine, serial number S-97-20938547__ to secure the payment and performance of the Debtor's obligations described as follows (the "Obligations"):

To make payments pursuant to the Note between
the parties, dated June 6, 2007.

Upon any default by the Debtor in the performance of any of the Obligations, the Creditor may declare all obligations of the Debtor immediately due and payable and shall have the remedies of a secured party under the Uniform Commercial Code enacted in the state the laws of which govern the terms of this agreement.

This agreement is executed by the parties under seal on __June 6, 2008__ .

Seller: Scrupulous Corporation   Buyer: FBN, Inc.

By:_*Henry Hardy*_____   By:_*Marcia Bender*_____
Henry Hardy, President   Marcia Bender, President

Attest:_*Calvin Collier*_____   Attest:_*Matthew G. Bender*_____
Calvin Collier, Secretary   Matthew G. Bender, Secretary

(Corporate Seal)   (Corporate Seal)

The **Sales Agreement** will be accompanied by a **Promissory Note**. See Chapter 8 for more information on promissory notes.

Bill of Sale   A **Bill of Sale** is like a deed for property other than real estate. See the sample below and the blank form in the appendix. (see form 29, p.179.) It is evidence that the buyer owns the property and that he or she bought it from the seller. It may also have some warranties from the seller, such as that the seller owned the property and had the right to sell it.

Sample of Form 29: Bill of Sale

BILL OF SALE

For valuable consideration, the receipt and sufficiency of which is hereby acknowledged, the undersigned hereby sells and transfers to _____FBN, Inc._____ the following:

1 Scrupulous TC III computer, serial number 229458326, and
1 Scrupulous SuperWriter Pro printer, serial number 492720-33927

The undersigned warrants and represents that it has good title to and full authority to sell and transfer the same and that the property is sold and transferred free and clear of all liens, claims, and encumbrances except: None.

Executed under seal on _____June 6, 2008_____.

Scrupulous Corporation

By: _____*Henry Hardy*_____
Henry Hardy, President

Attest:

_____*Calvin Collier*_____
Calvin Collier, Secretary

(Corporate Seal)

Some buyers may insist on a warranty that specifically includes an indemnity provision. You will note that form 29 in the appendix includes two **BILL OF SALE** forms, one like that on the previous page and the other containing the following indemnity provision:

> The undersigned warrants that, subject to the exceptions stated above, it will indemnify the Buyer, and defend title to the property, against the adverse claims of all persons.

VARIOUS CONTRACT WARRANTIES

Anyone who sells *goods* (which includes all kinds of merchandise and equipment) implies in so doing that he or she at least has title to the goods and the right to sell them.

Although the legal details that apply to implied and express warranties made by companies in the business of selling a particular item are beyond the scope of this book, a few words of warning may be helpful. If a seller is a merchant in the type of goods being sold, there are additional warranties implied under the Uniform Commercial Code, unless the seller disclaims them and sells the goods on an *as is* basis. If a merchant wants to go beyond implied warranties and make some specific promise about the nature or quality of the goods being sold, it is certainly possible to do so.

But be careful. If you are in the business of selling consumer goods, you may be subject to the *Magnuson-Moss Warranty Act* passed by Congress in 1975. The act does not prevent you from making promises, but requires specific disclosures if you do. Anything less than a *full warranty* (which means, among other things, that you promise to provide free repairs or replacement of defective parts) must be labeled *limited warranty*. Needless to say, most express warranties are limited warranties. If you want to give a warranty with a product you are in the business of selling, check with your lawyer to make sure you are really promising what you intend to and that you have done it correctly.

Sample Limited Warranty

LIMITED WARRANTY

The movement parts of your Scrupulous timepiece are warranted against defects in material and workmanship for five years to the initial consumer/owner from the date of purchase. All defective parts will be replaced with genuine factory parts at no charge for parts or labor. A handling charge of $8.00 will apply.

This Limited Warranty does not cover batteries, energy cells, case, crystal, strap, or bracelet. This Limited Warranty does not cover damage resulting from accident, misuse, abuse, dirt, water, or tampering.

This Limited Warranty gives you specific legal rights, and you may also have other rights that may vary from state to state. Except as otherwise required by law, this Limited Warranty is in lieu of all other warranties, conditions, guarantees, or representations, express or implied. Scrupulous Corporation shall not be liable for incidental, consequential, special, or indirect damages in connection with the product sold under this Limited Warranty or its use.

Sample Warranty of Title

The seller warrants and represents that it has good title to and full authority to sell and transfer the property being sold and that the property is sold and transferred free and clear of all liens and encumbrances.

Sample Disclaimer of Warranty

The seller disclaims any warranty of merchantability or fitness for a particular purpose. The property is sold in its present condition, "as is" and "where is."

CONSIGNMENT SALES

A *consignment sale* is one in which the owner gives something to another person for the purpose of selling it. The owner continues to own the item until it is actually sold, at which time the person in charge of selling it passes the purchase price on to the owner, usually subtracting a commission. The sample CONSIGNMENT SALES AGREEMENT is an agreement between the owner (the consignor) and the person in charge of selling the item (the consignee). (see form 28, p.177.)

Occasionally, the consignee may go bankrupt or have property taken to pay a judgment lien. To prevent this affecting the cosignor's property, consignors often require a financing statement (UCC-1) be filed so that there will be a public record of the consignor's ownership. (Also see the discussion and sample of financing statements in Chapter 8.)

Sample of Form 28: Consignment Sales Agreement

CONSIGNMENT SALE AGREEMENT

This agreement is made by and between _____Best Furniture, Inc._____ (the "Consignor") and ___Blanche Smith, d/b/a SalesMaster___ (the "Consignee").

1.   The Consignor and Consignee acknowledge and agree that the Consignor has provided the goods described below to Consignee for sale on a consignment basis, for the prices indicated, under the terms and conditions of this agreement:

(14)	Shelving units, Model #2433	$43.00 ea.
(6)	End tables, Model #2001	$48.00 ea.
(2)	Coffee tables, Model #2008	$61.00 ea.

2.   The Consignee agrees to use its best efforts to sell the goods, for cash, for the benefit of the Consignor and to account to the Consignor for such sales within _____90 days_____, delivering the sale proceeds to the Consignor, less commission, at the time of the accounting.

3.   The Consignee agrees to accept as its commission, in full payment for its performance under this agreement, an amount equal to __12__% of the gross sales price of the goods exclusive of any sales taxes.

4.   Any goods the Consignee is unable to sell may be returned to the Cosigner at the expense of the Cosignee. The Consignor may reclaim unsold goods at any time.

5. At the request of the Consignor, the Consignee agrees to execute financing statements perfecting the Consignor's claim of ownership of the goods.

IN WITNESS WHEREOF the parties have signed this agreement under seal on _December 18, 2008_.

Consignor: Best Furniture, Inc.   Consignee: Salesmaster

By: _*Stella Martin*_   By: _*Blanche Smith*_
Stella Martin, President   Blanche Smith, Owner
Best Furniture, Inc.   Blanche Smith, d/b/a
                                                   SalesMaster

EQUIPMENT RENTAL AGREEMENTS

Equipment leasing arrangements may really be an alternative method of financing the purchase of equipment. The lessee *leases* the equipment but expects to acquire ownership at the end of the lease term. The tax treatment of such arrangements is a complicated subject that cannot be dealt with here. The sample of form 39 that follows, **PERSONAL PROPERTY LEASE AGREEMENT**, is for a relatively short-term rental of equipment that will be returned to the lessor at the end of the term. (see form 39, p.199.)

Sample of Form 39: Personal Property Lease Agreement

PERSONAL PROPERTY LEASE AGREEMENT

This agreement is made by and between <u>Scrupulous Corporation</u> (the "Lessor") and <u>Scrupulous Associates</u> (the "Lessee").

1. The Lessor hereby leases to the Lessee, and the Lessee hereby leases from the lessor, beginning on <u>June 1, 2008</u> and terminating on <u>September 30, 2008</u>, the property described below (the "Property"):

CopyMate copier, Model #2500, Serial #6402748929328

2. The Lessee shall pay to the Lessor as rent the sum of $<u>100.00</u> per month payable in advance on or before the <u>1st</u> day of each month, the first such payment being due on <u>June 1, 2008</u>. Payment of rent shall be made to the Lessor at the following address:

201 Wacker Drive, Suite 622, Chicago, IL 60602

3. The Lessee agrees to use the Property in a careful manner and in compliance with applicable laws and regulations, and at the end of the lease term shall return the Property to the Lessor in the same condition as it was received by the Lessee, normal wear and tear excepted.

4. The Lessor shall not be liable for any liability, loss, or damage caused by the Property or its use that does not result directly and wholly from the negligence of the Lessor.

IN WITNESS WHEREOF the parties have signed this agreement under seal on <u>May 25, 2008</u>.

Lessor: Scrupulous Corporation

Lessee: Scrupulous Associates,
a general partnership

Henry Hardy
_____
Henry Hardy, President

Roberta Moore (Seal)
_____
Roberta Moore, Partner

Calvin Collier
_____
Calvin Collier, Secretary
(Corporate Seal)

_____

UNIFORM COMMERCIAL CODE TRANSACTIONS

The Uniform Commercial Code has been adopted by all states except Louisiana. The detailed requirements of the code are beyond the scope of this book; however, there are a couple of forms in the appendix you may find useful.

The Uniform Commercial Code sets forth certain actions you may take in the event that goods you purchase do not conform to the specifications or requirements of what you ordered. Basically, you may either reject the goods, or accept them on certain conditions. Either way, you need to officially notify the seller. There is a **NOTICE OF REJECTION OF NON-CONFORMING GOODS** in the appendix. (see form 30, p.181.) There is also a **NOTICE OF CONDITIONAL ACCEPTANCE OF NON-CONFORMING GOODS**. (see form 31, p.183.)

In form 30, you will need to describe or explain how the goods do not conform to what you ordered. In form 31, you will need to explain how the goods do not conform, and you will also need to spell out the terms under which you will accept the non-conforming goods (such as for a reduction in the price, some corrective action on the part of the seller, etc.). If the seller does not agree with your terms, you will then need to send a notice of rejection.

Sample of Form 30: Notice of Rejection of Non-Conforming Goods

Date: July 25, 2008

To: Slick Hand Cream Company
       248 Youthful Circle
       Norfolk, VA 23498

Re: Purchase order no. 25890A

We hereby reject the delivery of the goods specified in the above-mentioned purchase order. We received delivery on July 20, 2008 ; however, the goods do not conform to the specifications and requirements of our purchase order for the following reasons:

Our order was for 20 cases of Slick's Apple Scented Hand Cream. However, the shipment contained only Slick's Raspberry Scented Hand Cream.

We paid for the goods with check number 8903 , dated July 18, 2008 , in the sum of $350.00 . In the event you have not yet cashed this check, please return the check to us. If the check has been cashed, we hereby demand a refund of this amount. If we do not receive a refund within 14 days of the date of this Notice, we will take legal action for the refund.

Please notify us of your desires regarding the disposition of the goods at your expense. If we do not receive instructions within 14 days of the date of this Notice, we will not accept any responsibility for storage.

Please be advised that we reserve all rights available to us under the Uniform Commercial Code and any other applicable law.

SCRUPULOUS CORPORATION
Retail Division
3458 Storage Road
Center City, North Carolina 24890

James Procurer

James Procurer, Purchasing Manager

Sample of Form 31: Notice of Conditional Acceptance of Non-Conforming Goods

Date: July 25, 2008

To: Slick Hand Cream Company
      248 Youthful Circle
      Norfolk, VA 23498

Re: Purchase Order No. 25890A

You are hereby notified that the goods delivered to us on July 23, 2008 , pursuant to the above-mentioned purchase order, do not conform to the specifications and requirements of our purchase order for the following reasons:

Our order was for 20 cases of Slick's Apple Scented Hand Cream. However, the shipment contained only Slick's Raspberry Scented Hand Cream.

Although we are under no obligation to accept such non-conforming goods, we are willing to accept them on the following condition(s):

That you reduce the price for the goods by 20%.

If you do not notify us in writing that you are accepting these terms within 14 days of the date of this Notice, we will reject the goods and they will be returned to you at your expense.

Please be advised that we reserve all rights available to us under the Uniform Commercial Code and any other applicable law.

SCRUPULOUS CORPORATION
Retail Division
3458 Storage Road
Center City, North Carolina 24890

James Procurer
_____

James Procurer, Purchasing Manager

Sale and Purchase of a Business

There are many different methods of acquiring a business other than starting from scratch and building it. Corporate mergers, stock purchases, and asset purchases are the usual methods of acquiring an ongoing business. In a *stock purchase*, the acquirer will simply purchase most or all of the outstanding shares of a corporation. In the usual form, this means that the purchaser will negotiate the transaction with each existing shareholder of the target business. It works well if there is only one or a few shareholders, but it presents obvious difficulties if there are many.

Most states now allow a *share exchange* procedure in which the shareholders of the target company vote on whether to sell their shares as a group. The procedure for a share exchange is very much like that for a merger. A stock purchase can also be accomplished through a tender offer, which is a more complicated process. Stock purchases, share exchanges, and tender offers are regulated by federal and state securities laws, which are complex and difficult to navigate. You will need the services of an attorney if you are considering a share exchange or tender offer, so they will not be discussed in detail.

The term *stock transaction* or *stock purchase* specifically refers to the purchase of corporate shares. The same sort of transaction can be used to purchase a limited partnership or limited liability company, except that, instead of purchasing stock, the buyer purchases limited partnership interests or limited liability company memberships. Such acquisitions may involve particular problems, however. For example, when you purchase an LLC membership, you may be getting only the right to receive a share of the LLC's income without the right to participate in management. Make sure the transaction is reviewed by competent legal counsel to ensure that you are getting what you are paying for.

In an *asset purchase*, the acquirer buys most or all of the things owned by the target business and uses the assets to continue the business, leaving behind a shell more or less. The great thing about an asset purchase is that the buyer can pick and choose what it wants and leave behind the undesirable parts, including liabilities.

The tax implications of acquiring or disposing of a business are extremely complex, and these and other forms of acquisition should not be undertaken without ample expert advice.

A corporation involved in a stock or asset sale or purchase may require the approval of its shareholders. A share exchange will require the same sort of vote that a merger would. If a corporation sells all or substantially all its assets except in the ordinary course of business, that too requires shareholder approval.

STOCK TRANSACTIONS

The usual stock transaction involves one corporation buying all the outstanding shares of another from one or several shareholders. The procedure is not different in concept from the procedure you would use to buy a house. After looking over the purchase and deciding it is what you want, you negotiate a deal. Frequently there is a *letter of intent*, or *agreement in principle*, which is a sort of preliminary agreement laying out the basic terms of the deal. It may be a legally binding contract even though it is short and informal, so treat it with respect. The sample on the following page is a typical example, drafted with the protection of the buyer in mind, which specifically claims that it is not legally binding as a contract. Even so, it may have legal consequences, so do not sign it unless you mean it.

Once there is a letter of intent, your lawyers will negotiate a more detailed agreement that will cover the items mentioned in the letter of intent and many others besides.

Sample Letter of Intent Concerning *Stock Transaction*

Scrupulous Corporation of America ————————————————
400 West 61st Avenue, P.O. Box 19
New York, NY 10032

October 18, 2008

Franklin Distributors, Inc.
4250 Highway 40
New York, NY 10036

Dear Mr. Franklin:

This letter will confirm the understanding reached between you as the proposed seller and the undersigned as the proposed buyer on October 16, 2008. This letter is not a legally binding contract for the sale and purchase of shares, but only a description of the proposed arrangement by which the described transaction may take place.

Subject to the conditions stated in this letter, we have agreed in principle to buy and you have agreed to sell 100,000 common shares of Franklin Distributors, Inc. (the "Corporation"), being all the outstanding shares of the Corporation (the "Shares") for a purchase price of $2.50 per share for a total of $250,000.00 payable in cash at the closing. Closing of the transaction and transfer of the shares will take place not later than December 1, 2008, at a time and place to be agreed upon by the parties.

Our interest in and any obligations with regard to such purchase is subject to the following conditions:

1. Between the date of this letter and up to the closing date, the Corporation will provide us and our advisors, employees, and agents with an opportunity, at our expense, to perform a "due diligence" investigation and review of the Corporation's contracts, files, financial statements, accounts, stock record books, employee records, and such other books and records as we may see fit. If, during the course of such investigations, we should uncover information reasonably leading us to conclude that the value of the Corporation, as of the date of closing, is materially less than the proposed purchase price, we may withdraw from the proposed purchase.

2. Our agreement to purchase the Shares shall be subject to the drafting and execution of a definitive sale and purchase agreement satisfactory to our legal counsel and approved in final form by our Board of Directors. Such agreement shall contain customary representations and warranties given by you regarding the accuracy of the Corporation's financial statements, the legal status of the corporation and its outstanding shares, material litigation, ownership of assets, and other matters deemed of significance by us and our legal counsel in drafting such agreement.

3. Between the date of this letter and closing, the business of the Corporation will be conducted in the usual manner.

4. You and the Corporation will cooperate with us in any public announcements of the proposed sale and purchase deemed by our legal counsel to be required by law or otherwise desirable.

If this letter accurately states our understanding, please sign and date the enclosed copy and return it to us.

Very truly yours,

Scrupulous Corporation

By *Henry Hardy*

Henry Hardy, President

Accepted and agreed on: *10/20/08*
Franklin Distributors, Inc.

By *Milford Franklin*

Milford Franklin, President

ASSET TRANSACTIONS

In an asset transaction, instead of buying shares of stock, you are buying a list of individual items—desks, computers, paper clips, trucks, etc. It may be that some of these assets are transferable only by way of special documentation. For example, if you are buying the target's fleet of automobiles, you have to deal with the title documents peculiar to motor vehicles. If you are buying the target's real estate, deeds must be recorded, and if you are buying shares of stock that the target owns, the share certificates must be endorsed and the transfer recorded by the issuing corporation. So an asset transaction may involve a formidable stack of documents.

Nevertheless, the same basic documents involved in a typical stock transaction will be somewhere in the stack. The sample on the following page is the body of a letter of intent for an asset transaction.

Sample Letter of Intent Concerning *Asset Transaction*

Dear Mr. Franklin:

This letter will confirm the understanding reached between you as the proposed seller and the undersigned as the proposed buyer on October 16, 2008. This letter is not a legally binding contract for the sale and purchase of assets, but only a description of the proposed arrangement by which the described transaction may take place.

Subject to the conditions stated in this letter, we have agreed in principle to buy and you have agreed to sell all the assets (the "Assets") of Franklin Distributors, Inc. (the "Corporation"), for a purchase price of $250,000.00, payable in cash at the closing. Closing of the transaction and transfer of the assets will take place not later than December 1, 2008, at a time and place to be agreed upon by the parties.

Such sale and purchase is subject to the following conditions:

1.   Between the date of this letter and the closing date, the Corporation will provide us and our advisors, employees, and agents with an opportunity at our expense to perform a "due diligence" investigation and review of any and all of the Corporation's books and records as we may see fit. If such investigation uncovers information reasonably leading us to conclude that the value of the Assets, as of the date of closing, is materially less than the proposed purchase price, we may withdraw from the proposed purchase.

2.   Our agreement to purchase the Assets shall be subject to the drafting and execution of a definitive sale and purchase agreement satisfactory to our legal counsel and approved in final form by our Board of Directors. Such agreement shall contain a definitive list of the assets purchased and customary representations and warranties given by you regarding the value of the Assets and their ownership and other matters deemed of significance by us and our legal counsel in drafting such agreement.

3.   Between the date of this letter and closing, the business of the Corporation will be conducted in the usual manner.

4. You and the Corporation will cooperate with us in any public announcements of the proposed sale and purchase deemed by our legal counsel to be required by law or otherwise desirable.

If this letter accurately states our understanding, please sign and date the enclosed copy and return it to us.

Very truly yours,

Scrupulous Corporation

By _*Henry Hardy*_____
Henry Hardy, President

Accepted and agreed on: _*10/20/08*___
Franklin Distributors, Inc.

By _*Milford Franklin*_____
Milford Franklin, President

Bulk Sales   One of the advantages of an asset transaction previously mentioned is that the buyer can leave undesirable assets and liabilities of the seller behind and purchase only the assets the buyer really wants. This is in contrast to a merger or stock acquisition, in which the buyer acquires the target, warts and all, becoming responsible for the target's liabilities at the same time it acquires the target's assets. There is a danger, then, that in an asset deal, a corporation might keep its debts while giving up all the assets it could use to pay the debts, thus cheating its creditors.

Some states have enacted *bulk sales* statutes as a safeguard for creditors in such situations. The statutes require that a company selling most of its assets must give fair notice to its creditors so they can take steps to protect themselves. If the requirements of the statute are not followed precisely, the buyer will find itself responsible for the seller's debts whether it wants them or not. This is one big reason to consult a lawyer before completing such a transaction.

Dissenting Shareholders   As with mergers and share exchanges, shareholders of a corporation selling substantially all its assets will have *dissenters' rights*.

A *dissenter's right* is a dissenting corporate shareholder's right to have his or her shares purchased by the company at a fair price. A *dissenting shareholder* is one who votes no at the shareholders' meeting approving the asset transaction, and who follows other steps required by statute to become a dissenter.

Once the transaction is completed, a dissenter's shares will be purchased by the corporation for *fair value* and the dissenter will no longer be a shareholder. *Fair value* is a price the corporation and the dissenting shareholder agree to. If they cannot agree, then a court will decide what is a fair value.

A corporation involved in any activity giving rise to dissenters' rights must carefully follow the statutory procedure or risk substantial liability. Experienced legal counsel is needed. The same goes for a shareholder who wants to exercise his or her rights as a dissenter.

Borrowing and Lending Money

Sooner or later, almost every business will find a reason to borrow or lend money. A loan may be as simple as an oral agreement and a hand-shake, or as complex as an installment loan with a variable rate of interest secured by a mortgage on real estate. This chapter deals with typical loan documents, such as promissory notes, and some of their attributes.

PROMISSORY NOTES

A *promissory note* is a contractual promise to pay money. Often it is a promise to repay borrowed money, but it can also be a promise to pay the purchase price for property or services. Some promissory note forms appear on the following pages, but first the difference between *assigning* a note and *negotiating* a note must be considered.

Assignment and Negotiation

Most contracts are assignable by the parties. Some contracts (also called *instruments* or *negotiable instruments*) are also negotiable. *Negotiation* is a special kind of assignment.

The assignment of contractual rights was discussed in Chapter 1 of this book. Ordinarily when a party to a contract assigns or sells his or her rights under a contract, there is a very common sense rule that you cannot transfer away more rights than you own.

Example:

Suppose Johnny enters into a contract under which he promises to mow the neighbor's lawn for $25. In legal terms, Johnny has a duty to mow the lawn, and he has a right to receive payment of $25. His right to receive the $25 is conditional upon his performing the duty. That is, if he does not mow the lawn, Johnny has no right to get paid.

Now suppose Johnny wants to buy a new tire for his bicycle. He has no cash, so he trades his right to receive the $25 lawn mowing fee in exchange for the new tire. Now Johnny has a tire, and the former owner of the tire has a right to receive payment of $25 from Johnny's neighbor, but only if Johnny mows the neighbor's lawn.

If the lawn does not get mowed, the neighbor does not have to pay any money to the seller of the tire. Johnny transferred away his right to receive the $25, but the right was subject to Johnny's performance of his promise to mow the lawn. He could transfer only this conditional right to the seller of the tire. In legal terms, Johnny could not assign his right to receive $25 free of the condition, because that would be transferring away more than he owns.

Negotiability

Negotiability is a special quality of certain kinds of documents. If a document is *negotiable*, it means that the owner may be able to transfer away more rights than he or she owns. It would be the equivalent of Johnny's neighbor having to pay the $25 to the tire seller whether or not Johnny mowed the lawn. The purpose is to make *negotiable instruments*, such as notes and bank checks, as close to being a substitute for cash money as possible. If someone endorses a check to you, as endorsee, you do not want to have to worry about whether the endorser really did whatever the check paid for.

Example:

Suppose Elena is the owner of a restaurant, and she needs a new refrigerator for the restaurant kitchen. She buys the refrigerator and agrees to pay for it on an installment plan. As soon as she signs a promissory note for the payment of the refrigerator, the dealer assigns it to the bank, meaning that the dealer gets some amount of cash and the bank now has the right to collect Elena's monthly payments for itself.

Shortly after Elena installs the new refrigerator, it breaks down. Elena complains, but the refrigerator cannot be fixed. The bank comes to collect the next monthly payment on the installment plan, and Elena refuses to pay on grounds that the refrigerator was no good. If she owed the money to the refrigerator dealer, clearly Elena would not have to pay, because the dealer breached his contract to sell a functioning refrigerator. But she does not owe the dealer; she owes the bank. Does she have to pay or not?

The answer depends on the negotiability of the promissory note she signed. If the refrigerator dealer negotiated the promissory note to the bank, Elena would have to pay, because the bank would have taken the rights to payment free of Elena's defense that the refrigerator was no good. If the dealer merely assigned the note to the bank, then Elena would not have to pay, because the bank would have taken the right to receive payment subject to Elena's defense.

NOTE: *In Elena's example, the refrigerator was used as equipment in a business. If Elena had taken the refrigerator home to her private kitchen, it would be* consumer goods *and federal and state law would most likely protect Elena from having to pay the bank for a bad refrigerator.*

A note is *negotiable* if:

✪   the promise to pay the money is not subject to any conditions;

✪   the promise is written and signed;

✪   it is payable to a named person or a person to whom the note has been *negotiated* (sold) or to the *bearer* or *holder* of the note; and,

✪   it is to be paid either on a specified date or on the demand of the person to whom the debt is owed.

These requirements account for some of the odd language that notes and other negotiable instruments, such as checks, use. For example, the words *pay to the order of* mean that the person who owes the money has to pay it to the person named or to whomever that person orders it to be paid—that is, to whomever it has been negotiated. There are other kinds of contracts that create an obligation to repay money, but promissory notes are the most reliable and readily enforceable. See "Notice of Debt Assignments" on page 93.

Method of Payment

Promissory notes can be simple or quite complex, with many different arrangements for interest rates and repayment. The following sample of form 22 is an example of a completed **PROMISSORY NOTE** for repayment on demand of the holder of the note. This uses form 22 from the appendix, with the appropriate language typed in for this type of repayment. (see form 22, p.165.) The other samples of form 22 are examples of the language to be filled in on form 22 in the appendix for various other methods of repayment.

– Caution –

Do not sign duplicate copies of a **PROMISSORY NOTE**. Each signed note is an enforceable promise to pay the money referred to in the note. So if you sign three copies of the same note, you have promised to pay the same amount of money three times. Even machine copies of a note should be made before the note is signed (and the copy should not be signed, of course) so there will not be any mistakes.

Sample of Form 22: Promissory Note *for Payment on Demand*

PROMISSORY NOTE

$ 10,000.00   Date: July 1, 2008

    Scrupulous Corporation   hereby promises to pay to the order of   Roberta Moore   the sum of $ 10,000.00   with interest thereon from the date of this note to the date of payment at the rate of interest per annum as set forth below:

This note shall bear interest at the rate of 12% per annum on any unpaid balance. This note is payable upon demand of the holder made in writing to the undersigned at the address listed below.

    This note is due payable in full on   demand of the holder   , if not paid sooner. The principal and interest shall be payable when due at   400 West 61st Avenue,   P.O. Box 19, New York, NY 10032   or at a place of which the undersigned may be notified in writing by the holder of this note.

    This note is not assumable without the written consent of the lender. This note may be paid in whole or in part at any time prior without penalty. The borrower waives demand, presentment, protest, and notice. This note shall be fully payable upon demand of any holder in the event the undersigned shall default on the terms of this note or any agreement securing the payment of this note. In the event of default, the undersigned agrees to pay all costs of collection including reasonable attorney's fees.

    ❑ This note is given in payment for the purchase of personal property and is secured by a security interest in such property.

Scrupulous Corporation

By: *Henry Hardy*
Henry Hardy, President

Attest: *Calvin Collier*
Calvin Collier, Secretary
(Corporate Seal)

Sample of Form 22: Promissory Note *Due on Specific Date*

    This note shall bear interest at the rate of 12% per annum on any unpaid balance. This note is due a payable in full on   July 1, 2009   , if not paid sooner.

Sample of Form 22: Promissory Note *for Installment Payments*

This note shall bear interest at the rate of 12% per annum on any unpaid balance. The principal and interest shall be payable in equal monthly installments of $222.45 each, beginning on August 1, 2008, and continuing on the 1st day of each month thereafter.

Sample of Form 22: Promissory Note *for Balloon Payment*

This note shall bear interest at the rate of 12% per annum. The principal and interest shall be payable in equal monthly installments of $143.48 each, beginning on August 1, 2008, continuing on the 1st day of each month thereafter until August 1, 2008, at which time the entire balance shall become due and payable.

Interest Calculations

There must be an infinite number of ways to calculate interest on a loan. The previous four examples provide for a basic fixed rate. The following sample provides for the rate to increase each year. This might be used as an incentive for early repayment. Another method is to peg the rate to the prime rate of a designated bank.

Sample of Form 22: Promissory Note *for Increasing Interest Rate*

From the date of this note to the first anniversary of such date at the rate of 8%.

From the first anniversary of this note to the second anniversary at the rate of 10%.

From the second anniversary of this note to the third anniversary at the rate of 12%.

SECURING THE LOAN

If payment of a loan is to be secured by a lien on some piece of property, an agreement separate from the promissory note is needed. The sample of form 25 in Chapter 6 is an example of a **SECURITY AGREEMENT** creating a security interest in a piece of personal property. Regarding security interests in real property, see Chapter 5.

A security agreement establishes a relationship between the borrower and lender; that is, the borrower has designated some property as security and given the lender power to sell the property in satisfaction of the debt in case the borrower defaults. But what is to keep the borrower from selling the collateral to a third party before the loan is in default or before the lender has a chance to foreclose on the collateral? It would be unfair for an innocent third party purchaser of the collateral to lose the property he or she has paid good money for just because the borrower has breached his or her contract with the lender.

Protections

Such third parties do have some protection. One protection is the *financing statement* described in the following pages. It is a public document giving notice that the lender has a security interest in certain goods. Before you buy personal property, it may be advisable to check with the secretary of state and the local register of deeds to see whether such a statement has been filed. This is similar to a real property *title search*, one of the purposes of which is to reveal outstanding mortgages.

Purchasers of goods may have other protections making it unnecessary to check the record for financing statements. If you are a good faith purchaser of goods bought in the ordinary course of business, you take ownership of the goods free of the lender's security interest. This applies to the situation when you go to a store and buy the goods on sale there. This is an important rule, because obviously, business would come to a standstill if you had to check the public filings records every time you went into a store to buy a new dress or suit.

A financing statement also protects the lender. It does so by making sure that third parties will know—or at least have an opportunity to learn—that there is a security agreement in effect. This is called *perfecting* a security interest. One way to perfect a security interest is for the lender to take physical possession of the collateral as in a pawn shop transaction. Another way is for the lender to file a public notice of the security agreement on form UCC-1. A UCC-1 or *financing statement* is filed with some designated official and provides public notice that the property described in the notice serves as collateral for a loan. (See the sample on page 92.) UCC forms are generally standardized and look the same everywhere. The forms are available online, usually on the secretary of state's website for your state. Where the statement should be filed depends on the type of collateral and on state law. Your state will have a centralized filing system (usually in the office of the secretary of state), and a local filing system. If you are the seller, be sure you file in the right place. You may have to file in both places. If the collateral is a motor vehicle or boat, there will be a different system for recording security liens.

UCC-1 financing statements do not last forever. They expire after five years in most states. If the lender wants the security interest to continue beyond that time, it must file a continuation statement on form UCC-3, which is also the form used for amendment, termination, or assignment of security interests. An example of form UCC-3 appears later in this chapter.

Sample of UCC-1 Financing Statement

UCC FINANCING STATEMENT

FOLLOW INSTRUCTIONS (front and back) CAREFULLY

A. NAME & PHONE OF CONTACT AT FILER [optional]

B. SEND ACKNOWLEDGMENT TO: (Name and Address)

Scrupulous Corporation
400 West 61st Avenue
New York, NY 10032

THE ABOVE SPACE IS FOR FILING OFFICE USE ONLY

1. DEBTOR'S EXACT FULL LEGAL NAME - insert only one debtor name (1a or 1b) - do not abbreviate or combine names

1a. ORGANIZATION'S NAME			
FBN, Inc.			

OR

1b. INDIVIDUAL'S LAST NAME	FIRST NAME	MIDDLE NAME	SUFFIX

1c. MAILING ADDRESS	CITY	STATE	POSTAL CODE	COUNTRY
P.O. Box 27198	Fresno	CA	93706	USA

1d. SEE INSTRUCTIONS	ADD'L INFO RE ORGANIZATION DEBTOR	1e. TYPE OF ORGANIZATION	1f. JURISDICTION OF ORGANIZATION	1g. ORGANIZATIONAL ID #, if any
				☒ NONE

2. ADDITIONAL DEBTOR'S EXACT FULL LEGAL NAME - insert only one debtor name (2a or 2b) - do not abbreviate or combine names

2a. ORGANIZATION'S NAME			

OR

2b. INDIVIDUAL'S LAST NAME	FIRST NAME	MIDDLE NAME	SUFFIX

2c. MAILING ADDRESS	CITY	STATE	POSTAL CODE	COUNTRY

2d. SEE INSTRUCTIONS	ADD'L INFO RE ORGANIZATION DEBTOR	2e. TYPE OF ORGANIZATION	2f. JURISDICTION OF ORGANIZATION	2g. ORGANIZATIONAL ID #, if any
				☐ NONE

3. SECURED PARTY'S NAME (or NAME of TOTAL ASSIGNEE of ASSIGNOR S/P) - insert only one secured party name (3a or 3b)

3a. ORGANIZATION'S NAME			
Scrupulous Corporation			

OR

3b. INDIVIDUAL'S LAST NAME	FIRST NAME	MIDDLE NAME	SUFFIX

3c. MAILING ADDRESS	CITY	STATE	POSTAL CODE	COUNTRY
400 West 61st Avenue	New York	NY	10032	USA

4. This FINANCING STATEMENT covers the following collateral:

Scrupulous Model S-250 stamping machine, Serial #S-96-20938547

5. ALTERNATIVE DESIGNATION [if applicable]: ☐ LESSEE/LESSOR ☐ CONSIGNEE/CONSIGNOR ☐ BAILEE/BAILOR ☐ SELLER/BUYER ☐ AG. LIEN ☐ NON-UCC FILING

6. ☐ This FINANCING STATEMENT is to be filed [for record] (or recorded) in the REAL ESTATE RECORDS.   Attach Addendum   [if applicable]   **7.** Check to REQUEST SEARCH REPORT(S) on Debtor(s) [ADDITIONAL FEE]   [optional]   ☐ All Debtors ☐ Debtor 1 ☐ Debtor 2

8. OPTIONAL FILER REFERENCE DATA

International Association of Commercial Administrators (IACA)

FILING OFFICE COPY — UCC FINANCING STATEMENT (FORM UCC1) (REV. 05/22/02)

Notice of Debt Assignments

As explained at the beginning of this chapter, one of the important attributes of a **PROMISSORY NOTE** is its negotiability. When a note is *negotiated* (sold, endorsed, and delivered in the way specified by the Uniform Commercial Code), it is important for the new owner to notify the borrower that future payments should be made to him or her. See Chapter 1 for more information about the assignment of contracts and the need for appropriate notice. The following sample is such a notice to a debtor.

Sample Notice of Assignment of Debt

Notice of Assignment of Debt

To: FBN, Inc.

    You are hereby notified that Scrupulous Corporation has assigned and sold to National Service, Inc., its rights pursuant to your promissory note dated June 6, 2008, and that your debt in the amount of $30,000.00 is now owed to the undersigned. All future payments should be directed to the undersigned to insure credit for payment.

Peter J. Piper
_____
Peter J. Piper, President
National Service, Inc.
1423 W. 73rd Street
New York, NY 10034

Completion of Payments

Discharge of promissory note. Once a loan is completely paid, it is good practice for the original note to be returned to the borrower with a notation by the lender that it has been paid. Rather than destroy the original, the borrower should keep the original note with the lender's notation. That way you have written evidence that the lender has accepted final payment. The following sample, if written on the face of the note by an authorized agent of the lender, will cancel the note.

Sample Cancellation of Note

THIS NOTE WAS PAID AND SATISFIED IN FULL BY THE BORROWER ON MAY 23, 2008.

National Service, Inc.
By: _____*Peter J. Piper*_____
Peter J. Piper, President

Basic discharge of security interest. When a note is paid and the loan discharged, any related security interest is automatically discharged as well. There are some occasions on which a lender and borrower will agree to cancel a security arrangement even though the underlying debt has not been paid. For example, a new form of security may be substituted for the existing arrangement.

The following sample provides written evidence that the security interest has been discharged.

Sample Release of Security Interest

Discharge of Security Interest

FOR VALUE RECEIVED, the undersigned hereby releases and discharges a security interest granted by FBN, Inc., to the undersigned pursuant to a security agreement dated September 16, 2000. This discharge shall constitute a discharge of the obligation for which such security interest was granted.

This discharge was executed on November 22, 2008.

Scrupulous Corporation

By _Henry Hardy_
Henry Hardy, President

Discharge of UCC financing statement. If a UCC financing statement was filed, you will also need to file a UCC termination statement. In most states, form UCC-3 is a multipurpose form used for the termination, continuation, amendment, or assignment of a security interest. Filing the form as a termination statement will have the effect of clearing the UCC-1 financing statement from the record. The sample on the following page is the standard form. Like the UCC-1, you can download the form, including instructions and filing fee information, from your secretary of state's website.

Sample of UCC-3 Termination of Security Interest

UCC FINANCING STATEMENT AMENDMENT

FOLLOW INSTRUCTIONS (front and back) CAREFULLY

A. NAME & PHONE OF CONTACT AT FILER [optional]

B. SEND ACKNOWLEDGMENT TO: (Name and Address)

FBN, Inc.
P.O. Box 27198
Fresno, CA 93706

THE ABOVE SPACE IS FOR FILING OFFICE USE ONLY

1a. INITIAL FINANCING STATEMENT FILE #

96-25179

1b. This FINANCING STATEMENT AMENDMENT is to be filed [for record] (or recorded) in the REAL ESTATE RECORDS.

2. ☒ TERMINATION: Effectiveness of the Financing Statement identified above is terminated with respect to security interest(s) of the Secured Party authorizing this Termination Statement.

3. ☐ CONTINUATION: Effectiveness of the Financing Statement identified above with respect to security interest(s) of the Secured Party authorizing this Continuation Statement is continued for the additional period provided by applicable law.

4. ☐ ASSIGNMENT (full or partial): Give name of assignee in item 7a or 7b and address of assignee in item 7c; and also give name of assignor in item 9.

5. AMENDMENT (PARTY INFORMATION): This Amendment affects ☐ Debtor or ☐ Secured Party of record. Check only one of these two boxes.
Also check one of the following three boxes and provide appropriate information in items 6 and/or 7.

☐ CHANGE name and/or address: Give current record name in item 6a or 6b; also give new name (if name change) in item 7a or 7b and/or new address (if address change) in item 7c.   ☐ DELETE name: Give record name to be deleted in item 6a or 6b.   ☐ ADD name: Complete item 7a or 7b, and also item 7c; also complete items 7d-7g (if applicable).

6. CURRENT RECORD INFORMATION:

6a. ORGANIZATION'S NAME			
OR 6b. INDIVIDUAL'S LAST NAME	FIRST NAME	MIDDLE NAME	SUFFIX

7. CHANGED (NEW) OR ADDED INFORMATION:

7a. ORGANIZATION'S NAME			
OR 7b. INDIVIDUAL'S LAST NAME	FIRST NAME	MIDDLE NAME	SUFFIX

7c. MAILING ADDRESS	CITY	STATE	POSTAL CODE	COUNTRY

7d. TAX ID #: SSN OR EIN	ADD'L INFO RE ORGANIZATION DEBTOR	7e. TYPE OF ORGANIZATION	7f. JURISDICTION OF ORGANIZATION	7g. ORGANIZATIONAL ID #, if any ☐ NONE

8. AMENDMENT (COLLATERAL CHANGE): check only one box.

Describe collateral ☐ deleted or ☐ added, or give entire ☐ restated collateral description, or describe collateral ☐ assigned.

Scrupulous Corporation

9. NAME OF SECURED PARTY OF RECORD AUTHORIZING THIS AMENDMENT (name of assignor, if this is an Assignment). If this is an Amendment authorized by a Debtor which adds collateral or adds the authorizing Debtor, or if this is a Termination authorized by a Debtor, check here ☐ and enter name of DEBTOR authorizing this Amendment.

9a. ORGANIZATION'S NAME			
OR 9b. INDIVIDUAL'S LAST NAME	FIRST NAME	MIDDLE NAME	SUFFIX

10. OPTIONAL FILER REFERENCE DATA

FILING OFFICE COPY — NATIONAL UCC FINANCING STATEMENT AMENDMENT (FORM UCC3) (REV. 07/29/98)

DELINQUENT ACCOUNTS

If the buyer does not pay, there are various actions you may pursue. These range from a letter demanding payment to hiring a collection agency to filing a lawsuit. Some businesses send more than one demand letter before resorting to a lawsuit. One view is that lawsuits are expensive and time-consuming, and it is better to make numerous attempts to get payment voluntarily first. The other view is that multiple demand letters send a message to the debtor that you are not serious about collection and are merely making empty threats. If word gets around that you send one letter then sue, your debtors may take you more seriously.

The following sample of form 32 is a **DEMAND FOR PAYMENT**, which states that the next step is a lawsuit. (see form 32, p.185.) If you want to send more than one, you can simply modify it to delete or replace the language threatening a lawsuit, and indicate that it is a "Second Notice," "Third Notice," etc. The form as it is can then be designated the "Final Notice."

Sample of Form 32: Demand Letter

DEMAND FOR PAYMENT

Date: February 3, 2009

To: NSF Corporation
        52 S. First Street
        St. Louis, MO

Your account is delinquent in the amount of $ 4,680.86 .

Please be advised that in the event we do not receive payment in full within   14   days of the date of this notice, we will initiate collection proceedings against you without further notice. If such proceedings are initiated, you will also be responsible for pre-judgment interest, attorney's fees, court costs, and any and all other costs of collection. Collection proceedings may also adversely affect your credit rating.

If full payment has already been sent, please disregard this notice.

Please contact the undersigned if you have any questions.

Henry Hardy
_____
Henry Hardy, President
Scrupulous Corporation

If you decide to hire a collection agency, you can use the **NOTICE OF ASSIGNMENT OF ACCOUNT FOR COLLECTION** in the appendix to notify the debtor. (see form 34, p.189.) The sample of form 34 is completed as follows.

Sample of Form 34: Notice of Assignment of Account for Collection

---

NOTICE OF ASSIGNMENT OF ACCOUNT FOR COLLECTION

Date: <u>February 19, 2009</u>

To: NSF Corporation
           52 S. First Street
           St. Louis, MO

Please be advised that your delinquent account has been assigned for collection to the following collection agent: <u>Debt Collection Associates, Inc., 415 Strongarme Street, St. Louis, MO</u>. The amount assigned is based upon the following amount(s):

    $1,795.45, representing the amount owed for goods
    delivered pursuant to contract dated October 1,
    2008, plus accrued interest.

Please contact the above-mentioned collection agent regarding this notice and all future payments on this account.

                          Henry Hardy
                          _____
                          Henry Hardy, President
                          Scrupulous Corporation

Filing a Lawsuit

If you wish to file suit yourself, you should either hire a lawyer or look for a self-help law book appropriate for your state and the amount of your claim. Each state's court system usually has divisions based upon the type and the amount of the claim. For example, there may be a small claims court, a landlord/tenant court, etc.

chapter 9

Avoiding Liability and Settling Disputes

PROTECTING AGAINST LIABILITY BEFORE IT ARISES

Disclaimers of Liability

It is not unusual that a business will undertake something that everyone recognizes could go wrong, causing an injury. When all parties go into a contract with eyes open, fully informed, and understanding the risks, it is only fair that the person who bears potential liability have the ability to bargain away that risk. A **WAIVER AND ASSUMPTION OF RISK** is an acknowledgment by the customer who may be injured in a risky undertaking that he or she is aware of the risks and undertakes them willingly, releasing the business of liability for any resulting injury. (see form 54, p.245.) There is a sample on page 101.

How far can you go? As a rule of thumb, the person who agrees to a disclaimer such as the following assumes only the risks that are specified in the release or the ones that are reasonably foreseeable.

Example:

Suppose the company is in the business of renting parachutes to skydivers. A skydiver may reasonably foresee that, no matter how good the equipment is, a jump may go wrong. Knowing this, he or she may be expected to release the equipment renter from liability for injuries resulting from the jump. But does that include a release from liability if the equipment company negligently employs a parachute packer who gets drunk and does a poor job of preparing the equipment or fails to notice a fatal rip in the parachute's fabric? Probably not. But what if the release specifically states that the renter will not be responsible for torn or poorly packed parachutes prepared by drunken workers? Would the release be valid? Maybe, but who would knowingly sign such a thing?

A disclaimer such as this should be viewed as a sort of warning sign saying, "Here are the things that could go wrong. We are warning you about them in advance and letting you know we cannot be responsible for such things, because we cannot control them. You are responsible for your own injuries if you do this act." A disclaimer will have a chance of being effective only if the person who agrees to it has a fair chance to read and understand it. A disclaimer will not help you if you try to disguise it or hide it.

The sample of form 54 on the following page is a **WAIVER AND ASSUMPTION OF RISK**, which an individual customer will sign agreeing to assume the full risk for the use of certain facilities and for engaging in certain activities. The customer acknowledges that he or she is aware of the dangers inherent in the activity, and agrees to release the business from liability for injuries or damages that may result.

Sample of Form 54: Waiver and Assumption of Risk

WAIVER AND ASSUMPTION OF RISK

I, _____, hereby voluntarily sign this Waiver and Assumption of Risk in favor of _____Deep-C Divers, Inc._____ (the "Company"), fully waiving and releasing the Company from any and all claims for personal injury, property damage, or death that may result from my use of the Company's facilities or property, or from my participation in the following activities or instruction ("activities"):

> SCUBA diving and snorkeling, including, but not limited to, instruction from the company's employees, and use of the Company's swimming pool, boat, dock, and diving and snorkeling equipment.

I sign this Waiver and Assumption of Risk in consideration of the opportunity to use the Company's facilities or property, receive instruction from the Company and its employees, or to participate in Company-sponsored activities as described above.

I acknowledge and understand that there are dangers and risks associated with the activities described above, which have been fully explained to me. I fully assume the dangers and risks, and agree to use my best judgment in engaging in those activities and to follow the safety instructions provided.

I am a competent adult, aged _____, and I freely and voluntarily assume the risks associated with the activities described above.

Dated: _____

Witness: _____   _____

Name: _____
Address: _____
_____
Telephone: _____

In case of emergency, please contact:
Name: _____
Address :_____
_____
Relationship: _____
Telephone: _____

The sample of form 37 is a contract under which a corporation agrees to provide services as an independent contractor to a customer. It warns the customer of dangers inherent in the service to be performed, and the customer agrees to release the business from liability for injuries or damages that may result from the performance of the services. (see form 37, p.195.)

Sample of Form 37: Contract for Company's Services with Disclaimer and Release from Liability

---

CONTRACT FOR COMPANY'S SERVICES

This agreement is made between _____Scrupulous Corporation_____ (the "Company") and ___Developers, Inc.___, (the "Customer"). The Company and the Customer agree as follows:

1.   The Company will provide the following services to the Customer under the terms and conditions of this agreement:

Removal and disposal of one underground storage tank.

2.   The Company agrees to perform such services diligently, using its best efforts and providing competent personnel and adequate time to complete the work to professional standards of high quality. The Company may perform such services at the times and locations as may be agreed by the parties.

3.   As payment for the completed services described above, and in addition to the release provided in paragraph 5 below, the Customer shall pay to the Company the sum of $_1,750.00_ payable in the following manner:

50% upon commencement of work, and the balance upon completion.

4.   The services to be provided by the Company pursuant to this agreement shall begin not later than __May 1, 2008__ and shall be completed not later than __May 15, 2008__.

5.   DISCLAIMER OF LIABILITY AND RELEASE BY CUSTOMER—READ CAREFULLY: The Company has informed the Customer, and the Customer acknowledges having been informed that the performance of the services described above involves certain inherent risks and dangers including, but not limited to, the following: Leakage or spillage of material remaining in tank, and subsidence of adjacent ground and roadway.

THE COMPANY DISCLAIMS ALL LIABILITY FOR DAMAGES AND INJURIES THAT MAY RESULT FROM ALL RISKS REFERRED TO IN THIS PARAGRAPH, and the Customer, having been so informed, in further consideration of the Company's willingness to provide such services, hereby releases, discharges, and acquits the Company, and its employees, agents, successors, and assigns, from any and all claims, actions, suits, or liabilities that may arise as a result of or in connection with the performance of the services not resulting directly and wholly from the negligence of the Company, its agents, and its employees.

6. The parties agree that no employer-employee relationship is created by this agreement, but that the relationship of the Company to the Customer shall be that of an independent contractor.

IN WITNESS WHEREOF the parties have signed this agreement under seal on __April 25,__ __2008__.

Scrupulous Corporation   Developers, Inc.

By: _____*Henry Hardy*_____   By: _____*Ronald Bumpp*_____

Henry Hardy, President   Ronald Bumpp, President

Indemnification   While the disclaimer and release assures the company it will not be liable for certain damages, it does nothing to protect the company from liabilities that may nevertheless arise, either because the disclaimer is not broad enough or because the liabilities are such that they cannot be reasonably disclaimed. That is the purpose of an **INDEMNIFICATION AGREEMENT** such as in the sample below. (see form 62, p.261.) Remember that an indemnification is of no value if the indemnifier (*indemnitor*) has no funds to pay it with, so be careful who signs the agreement. You may want it signed by a corporation and also the shareholders, if you can get it.

Sample of Form 62: Agreement for Indemnification

INDEMNIFICATION AGREEMENT

In exchange for <u>the Company allowing use of its property by the undersigned as described below</u> and other valuable consideration, the receipt and sufficiency of which is hereby acknowledged, the undersigned hereby agrees to indemnify and hold <u>Scrupulous Corporation</u> (the "Company") harmless from any claim, action, liability, or suit arising out of or in any way connected with the following: the operation by Unified Charities, Inc., and CarniProductions, Inc., of a charity-benefit carnival, including, but not limited to, the operation of amusement rides, food concessions, and fireworks displays on the Company's property on February 14 and 15, 2009, including setup on February 13, 2009, and teardown on February 16, 2009.

In the event any claim reasonably believed by the Company to be subject to indemnification under this agreement is asserted against the Company, the Company will provide timely notice of such claim to the undersigned. The undersigned will thereafter, at its own expense, defend and protect the Company against such claim. Should the undersigned be unable or fail to so defend the Company, the Company shall have the right to defend or settle such claim, and the undersigned shall reimburse the Company for all settlements, judgments, fees, costs, expenses, and payments, including reasonable attorney's fees, incurred by the Company in connection with the discharge of such claim.

This agreement shall be binding upon the parties, and upon their heirs, executors, personal representatives, administrators, and assigns.

IN WITNESS WHEREOF the parties have signed this agreement under seal on <u>January 12, 2009</u>.

Unified Charities, Inc.

James Gooddeed
_____
James Gooddeed, President

Marcy Hopewell
_____
Marcy Hopewell, Secretary
(Corporate Seal)

CarniProductions, Inc.

Barnum N. Bayley
_____
Barnum N. Bayley, President

Buffy Ringling
_____
Buffy Ringling, Secretary
(Corporate Seal)

DISCHARGING LIABILITY AFTER IT ARISES

A *liability* is a debt owed. Like other debts, liabilities of tort (personal injury) or contract can be discharged in various ways, including the payment of money or promise to pay money. The sample of form 55 is a **GENERAL RELEASE** from all liabilities that the person released may owe to the signer. (see form 55, p.247.) The sample of form 56 is a **SPECIFIC RELEASE** limited to matters related to a specific event or contract. (see form 56, p.249.) In the sample **MUTUAL RELEASE** on page 105, the parties release each other from liabilities. (see form 57, p.251.)

Sample of Form 55: General Release of Liability

GENERAL RELEASE

In exchange for the sum of $10.00 and other valuable consideration, the receipt and sufficiency of which is hereby acknowledged, the undersigned hereby forever releases, discharges, and acquits Nationwide Carrier Corporation , and [its/his/her] successors, assigns, heirs, and personal representatives, from any and all claims, actions, suits, agreements, or liabilities in favor of or owed to the undersigned, existing at any time up to the date of this release.

IN WITNESS WHEREOF, the undersigned has executed this release under seal on May 8, 2008.

Scrupulous Corporation

By: *Henry Hardy*

Henry Hardy, President

Attest:
Calvin Collier

Calvin Collier, Secretary

(Corporate Seal)

Sample of Form 56: Specific Release of Liability

SPECIFIC RELEASE

In exchange for the sum of $10.00 and other valuable consideration, the receipt and sufficiency of which is hereby acknowledged, the undersigned hereby forever releases, discharges, and acquits Scrupulous Corporation , and [its/his/her] successors, assigns, heirs, and personal representatives, from any and all claims, actions, suits, agreements, or liabilities arising out of or related to:

any and all injuries and damages sustained by the undersigned, pursuant to the undersigned slipping and falling at the premises of Scrupulous Corporation on July 4, 2008.

IN WITNESS WHEREOF, the undersigned has executed this release under seal on August 28, 2008.

Justin Cayce

Justin Cayce

Sample of Form 57: Mutual Release of Liability

MUTUAL RELEASE

In exchange for the sum of $10.00 and other valuable consideration, the receipt and sufficiency of which is hereby acknowledged, the undersigned hereby forever release, discharge, and acquit each other, and their successors, assigns, heirs, and personal representatives, from any and all claims, actions, suits, agreements, or liabilities arising out of or related to: the contract executed by and between the parties on March 3, 2008.

IN WITNESS WHEREOF, the undersigned have executed this release under seal and by authority of their respective boards of directors as of October 27, 2008.

Western Distributors, Inc.

Jackson Miller
_____
Jackson Miller, President

David Jones
_____
David Jones, Secretary
(Corporate Seal)

Mountain Packaging,
a general partnership
Marilyn Kim
_____
Marilyn Kim, general partner

Mechanic's and Materialmen's Liens

Your state will have a statute that protects various workers from customers who do not pay. If you take your car in for repairs and then refuse to pay for the work done, the mechanic will have an automatic statutory *lien* on the vehicle for the amount of the repairs. If you persist in not paying, this means the mechanic can sell your car and apply the proceeds to the outstanding bill. The same is true of building contractors and suppliers.

It frequently becomes important for such automatic liens to be released (and proven in writing to be released) so that, for example, a new house can be sold free of any such liens. The sample of form 60 is an example of a **RELEASE OF LIENS**. (see form 60, p.257.) Presented to the purchaser, it will show that the building is free of any such liens from the contractor or supplier who signs it. If a lien has already been recorded, it will be necessary to use a form that refers to the book and page (or other appropriate recording information used in your state) where the lien was recorded.

Sample of Form 60: Release of Lien

REALEASE OF LIEN

The undersigned [sub]contractor has furnished construction materials and/or labor in connection with repairs or construction at the property described as: __9834 W. Washington Ave.,__ __St. Paul, MN__ (hereinafter called the "Premises"). The undersigned hereby releases all liens and rights to file liens against the Premises for any and all such materials or services provided through the date of this release.

The date of this release is __January 2, 2009__.

Contractor/Subcontractor:
Carl Nales, d/b/a Carl the Carpenter

Carl Nales
Carl Nales

Agreements Not to Bring Lawsuits

There is a difference between (1) agreeing that one person has no further claim of liability against another and (2) promising that, although there may be a claim, the person will not bring a lawsuit based on it. The former is a release, and the latter is a covenant not to sue. Once a claim has been released, it no longer exists and (unless there has been fraud involved) cannot be revived. But if you promise not to sue on a claim, the claim does not go away—you have just promised not to try to enforce it. If the promise not to sue goes away, the claim is still there, ready to be enforced.

If a claimant receives cash in an agreed settlement of the claim, it is appropriate to give a release. There will never be any need to enforce a debt that has been fully paid. If you only have a promise to pay something in the future, such as a promissory note, then maybe a covenant not to sue is appropriate. The claimant promises not to bring a lawsuit on the claim as long as the note is not in default.

Sample of Form 58: Covenant Not to Sue

COVENANT NOT TO SUE

This agreement is made by and between _____Justin Cayce_____ (the "Covenantor"), for [itself/himself/herself] and for its heirs, legal representatives, and assigns, and _____Scrupulous Corporation_____ (the "Covenantee").

1. In exchange for the Covenantor's covenant herein, the Covenantee _promises and agrees to pay all of the Covenantor's medical bills and $50 per day for lost wages arising out of injuries Covenantor received on July 4, 2008, at the Covenantee's premises.

2. In exchange for the consideration stated in paragraph 1 above, the receipt and sufficiency of which is hereby acknowledged by the Covenantor, the Covenantor covenants with the Covenantee that it will not institute any suit or action at law or in equity against the Covenantee by reason of any claim the Covenantor now has or may hereafter acquire related to: _injuries Covenantor received on July 4, 2008, at the Covenantee's premises_.

This agreement was executed by the parties under seal on _August 15, 2008_.

Covenantor: Covenantee:

                                          Scrupulous Corporation

Justin Cayce
_____
Justin Cayce

                                      Henry Hardy
                                      _____
                                      Henry Hardy, President

                                            Calvin Collier
                                        _____
                                      Calvin Collier, Secretary

                                        (Corporate Seal)

Judgments   If you already have a court *judgment* against you, it will eventually become necessary to get released from the judgment, either because you have paid it or because you have reached some kind of agreement with the person or company with the judgment against you. The sample of form 59 is an example of a **RELEASE OF JUDGMENT**. (see form 59, p.255.) You will need to complete the top portion of the form so that it matches what is on the judgment itself. This will typically include an identification of the court, the names of the parties, and a case number. You should also check to be sure the form you prepare complies with the requirements of your state and county for recording.

Sample of Form 59: Release of Judgment

IN THE CIRCUIT COURT OF THE STATE OF OREGON
THE COUNTY OF CLACKAMAS

Oregon City Manufacturing, Inc.,	)	
	)	
Plaintiff,	)	
	)	
v.	)	Case No. 95-9482
	)	
Scrupulous Corporation,	)	
	)	
Defendant.	)	
	)	

RELEASE OF JUDGMENT

The Plaintiff, <u>Oregon City Manufacturing, Inc.</u>, hereby acknowledges that the judgment in this action has been fully satisfied by the Defendant, <u>Scrupulous Corporation</u>, and hereby releases and discharges said Defendant from any and all further liability for said judgment.

Dated: <u>October 23, 2008</u>   .

Oregon City Manufacturing, Inc.

By:_*Henry Hardy*_____
Henry Hardy, President

SETTLING DISPUTES WITHOUT GOING TO COURT

There is no need to recite horror stories about going to court. It is expensive, slow, and chancy. In recent years, various means of *alternative dispute resolution* have become popular. Used correctly, the alternative dispute resolution procedures of *arbitration* or *mediation* can be much more efficient than litigation at settling disputes between parties who cannot come to an agreement on their own.

Arbitration

An *arbitrator* is a person who, like an umpire or judge, has the power to decide. The disputants, either by themselves or with the assistance of lawyers, present their arguments to the arbitrator, agreeing in advance to abide by his or her decision. It is a kind of private court system in which the parties get to choose the judge and make their own rules about procedure and evidence.

Mediation

A *mediator* has no power to decide. A mediator is a neutral party who acts as a go between to help the parties reach their own compromises and agreements. You might think that a mediator would be useless—if the parties cannot agree by themselves, why would they suddenly be able to do so with the help of a mediator who has no power to make decisions? Nevertheless, it frequently works. And it has an advantage over both litigation and arbitration. In court or arbitration, you put the results in the hands of outsiders. They may be fair decision makers, but it is still like giving them a signed, blank settlement agreement. The judge or arbiter gets to fill in the terms any way he or she wants. In mediation, the only people who can decide are the parties themselves. They keep complete control over the process.

The samples on the following page are clauses to be inserted in a contract by which the parties agree that any disputes to arise will be arbitrated. The first provides for arbitration under the rules of an organization that provides arbitration services. There are many such organizations, the most prominent one being the American Arbitration Association, which provides such services around the country. The second provides for arbitrators to be appointed by the parties without being overseen by such an organization.

Sample Contract Clause for Arbitration of Disputes; *Organization Rules*

> The parties agree that any controversy, claim, or dispute arising out of or related to this agreement or any breach of this agreement shall be submitted to arbitration by and according to the applicable rules of the American Arbitration Association and that judgment upon an award rendered by the arbitrator may be entered in any court having jurisdiction.

Sample Contract Clause for Arbitration of Disputes; *Arbitrator Selected by Parties*

> The parties agree that any controversy, claim, or dispute arising out of or related to this agreement or any breach of this agreement shall be submitted to arbitration. Such arbitration shall take place in Denver, Colorado , or at such other place as may be agreed upon by the parties. The parties shall attempt to agree on one arbitrator. If they are unable to so agree, then each party shall appoint one arbitrator and those appointed shall appoint a third arbitrator. The expenses of arbitration shall be divided equally by the parties. The prevailing party ❑ shall ☒ shall not be entitled to reasonable attorney's fees. The arbitrators shall conclusively decide all issues of law and fact related to the arbitrated dispute. Judgment upon an award rendered by the arbitrator may be entered in any court having jurisdiction.

The sample of form 53 on the following page is to be used after a dispute has arisen and is an agreement to submit the disagreement to arbitration, called an **ARBITRATION AGREEMENT**. (see form 53, p.243.) The sample on page 112 is a **MEDIATION AGREEMENT**. (see form 52, p.241.) Form 52 provides a fair means of selecting arbitrators. Form 53 presumes that the parties can agree on a mediator, which is usually easy to do since the mediator has no decision-making power. Besides, if you cannot even agree on a mediator, mediation probably will not be successful. These days there are trained arbitrators, mediators, and arbitration and mediation organizations in most areas. You can locate them through your lawyer or by calling your local or state bar association.

Sample of Form 53: Arbitration Agreement

ARBITRATION AGREEMENT

This Arbitration Agreement is made this __12th__ day of __October__, __2008__, by and between __Western Distributors, Inc.__ and __Mountain Packaging__, who agree as follows:

1. The parties agree that any controversy, claim, or dispute arising out of or related to:

    the contract executed by and between the parties
    on March 3, 2008,

shall be submitted to arbitration. Such arbitration shall take place at __7635 Red Rocks Hwy.,__ __Denver, CO__, or at such other place as may be agreed upon by the parties.

2. The parties shall attempt to agree on one arbitrator. If they are unable to so agree, then each party shall appoint one arbitrator and those appointed shall appoint a third arbitrator.

3. The expenses of arbitration shall be divided equally by the parties.

4. The arbitrators shall conclusively decide all issues of law and fact related to the arbitrated dispute. Judgment upon an award rendered by the arbitrator may be entered in any court having jurisdiction.

5. The prevailing party ❑ shall ☒ shall not be entitled to reasonable attorney's fees.

Western Distributors, Inc.   Mountain Packaging, a general partnership

Wanda Miller   *Marilyn Kim*
Wanda Miller, President   Marilyn Kim, general partner

Attest: *Martin Miller*
Martin Miller, Secretary
(Corporate Seal)

Sample of Form 52: Mediation Agreement

MEDIATION AGREEMENT

The undersigned parties are engaged in a dispute regarding <u>the contract between the</u> <u>parties dated February 12, 2008</u>. We hereby agree to submit such dispute to mediation by <u>Neighborhood Mediation Services</u> and that all matters resolved in mediation shall be reduced to a binding written agreement signed by the parties. The costs of mediation shall be borne equally by the parties.

Dated: <u>August 8, 2008</u>.

Scrupulous Corporation

Marketing Associates,
a general partnership

<u>*Henry Hardy*</u>

Henry Hardy, President

<u>*Murray Madison*</u>

Murray Madison,
general partner

Forms

This appendix contains blank forms for you to tear out and use. It is suggested that you photocopy the forms for use, leaving those in the book to photocopy again for future use. These forms can also be modified to fit your specific needs.

– Caution –

Lines are provided for signatures. The signature format will vary depending upon whether it is an individual, partnership, or corporation that is signing. There may be more lines than you need on the forms. If so, just ignore the extra lines. Be sure to add the notation "(Seal)" after an individual's signature or the signature of a partner who is signing for a partnership. If the person is signing for a partnership or corporation, you will need to type in the name of the partnership or corporation several lines above the signature line, add the word "By" on the signature line, and type in the signer's name and title just below the signature line. If the corporate secretary or assistant secretary is attesting to the signature of the office, you will need to add the word "Attest:" to the appropriate signature line, and type in the person's name and title just below that signature line. For more information to help you determine the proper signature format, refer to the section in Chapter 1 on "Signatures."

The requirements for notary public acknowledgments vary from state to state. Some states just require a simple statement that the person signed before the notary, some require the notary to see some form of identification and to keep a record, and others require the document itself to state what form of identification was produced. For the forms in this book, a more detailed format was used. It may exceed what is required in your state, or something may need to be changed or added. The notary in your state should know the requirements, and can modify the form if necessary to comply with legal requirements.

BASIC CONTRACT FORMS

EMPLOYEES, INDEPENDENT CONTRACTORS, AGENTS, AND PARTNERS

BORROWING AND LENDING

BUYING AND SELLING GOODS AND SERVICES

RENTING REAL OR PERSONAL PROPERTY

COPYRIGHTS AND OTHER INTELLECTUAL PROPERTY

AVOIDANCE OF LIABILITY AND SETTLEMENT OF DISPUTES

This page intentionally blank.

CONTRACT

THIS AGREEMENT is entered into by and between _____
_____ (hereafter referred to as _____)
and _____ (hereafter referred
to as _____). In consideration of the mutual promises made
in this agreement and other valuable consideration, the receipt and sufficiency of
which is acknowledged, the parties agree as follows:

The following addenda, dated the same date as this agreement, are incorporated in, and made a part of, this agreement:

❏ None.

This agreement shall be governed by the laws of _____.

If any part of this agreement is adjudged invalid, illegal, or unenforceable, the remaining parts shall not be affected and shall remain in full force and effect.

This agreement shall be binding upon the parties, and upon their heirs, executors, personal representatives, administrators, and assigns. No person shall have a right or cause of action arising out of or resulting from this agreement except those who are parties to it and their successors in interest.

This instrument, including any attached exhibits and addenda, constitutes the entire agreement of the parties. No representations or promises have been made except those that are set out in this agreement. This agreement may not be modified except in writing signed by all the parties.

IN WITNESS WHEREOF the parties have signed this agreement under seal on _____.

_____   _____

_____   _____

Page _____ of _____ pages.

ADDENDUM TO CONTRACT

Addendum No. _____

    The following terms are a part of the Contract, dated _____,
by and between _____ and
_____:

This page intentionally blank.

AMENDMENT TO CONTRACT

For valuable consideration, the receipt and sufficiency of which is acknowledged by each of the parties, this agreement amends a Contract dated _____, between _____ and _____, relating to _____.
This contract amendment is hereby incorporated into the Contract.

Except as changed by this amendment, the Contract shall continue in effect according to its terms. The amendments herein shall be effective on the date this document is executed by all parties.

IN WITNESS WHEREOF the parties have signed this agreement under seal on _____.

_____   _____

_____   _____

This page intentionally blank.

ASSIGNMENT OF CONTRACT

FOR VALUE RECEIVED the undersigned (the "Assignor") hereby assigns, transfers, and conveys to _____ (the "Assignee") all the Assignor's rights, title, and interests in and to a contract (the "Contract") dated _____, between _____ and _____.

The Assignor hereby warrants and represents that the Contract is in full force and effect and is fully assignable.

The Assignee hereby assumes the duties and obligations of the Assignor under the Contract and agrees to hold the Assignor harmless from any claim or demand thereunder.

The date of this assignment is _____.

IN WITNESS WHEREOF this agreement is signed by the parties under seal.

Assignor: Assignee:

_____   _____

_____   _____

This page intentionally blank.

NOTICE OF BREACH OF CONTRACT

Date: _____

To:

Dear Sir or Madam:

We refer to a contract dated _____ (the "Contract") pursuant to which you have obligated yourself to:

You have breached your duties under the Contract in that you have failed to:

We demand that you cure such default promptly. In the event that you fail to do so within _____ days of the date of this letter, we will refer the matter to attorneys for immediate action.

Sincerely,

This page intentionally blank.

TERMINATION OF CONTRACT

Date: _____

The undersigned have entered into a contract dated _____ (the "Contract") for the purpose of:

The undersigned acknowledge that, by their mutual agreement, the Contract is hereby terminated without further recourse by either party.

The termination of the Contract shall be effective on (date) _____.

_____

By: _____

_____

By: _____

This page intentionally blank.

APPLICATION FOR EMPLOYMENT

We consider applicants for all positions without regard to race, color, religion, sex, national origin, age, marital or veteran status, the presence of a non-job-related medical condition or handicap, or any other legally protected status.

Proof of citizenship or immigration status will be required upon employment.

(PLEASE TYPE OR PRINT)

Position Applied For   Date of Application

Last Name   First Name   Middle Name or Initial

Address   *Number*   *Street*   *City*   *State*   *Zip Code*

Telephone Number(s) [indicate home or work]   Social Security Number

Date Available:_____   Are you available: ☐ Full Time   ☐ Part Time
                                                          ☐ Weekends

Have you been convicted of a felony within the past 7 years?   ☐ Yes   ☐ No

Conviction will not necessarily disqualify an applicant from employment.

If yes, attach explanation.

Education

	High School	Undergraduate	Graduate
School Name & Location			
Years Completed	1 2 3 4	1 2 3 4	1 2 3 4
Diploma/Degree			
Course of Study			

State any additional information you feel may be helpful to us in considering your application (such as any specialized training; skills; apprenticeships; honors received; professional, trade, business, or civic organizations or activities; job-related military training or experience; foreign language abilities; etc.)

_____

_____

_____

_____

Employment Experience

Start with your present or last job. Include any job-related military service assignments and voluntary activities. You may exclude organizations that indicate race, color, religion, gender, national origin, handicap, or other protected status.

1.

Employer Name & Address	Dates Employed	Job Title/Duties
	Hourly Rate/Salary	
May we contact this employer? ❑ Yes ❑ No	Hours Per Week	
Employer Phone		
Supervisor		
Reason for Leaving		

2.

Employer Name & Address	Dates Employed	Job Title/Duties
	Hourly Rate/Salary	
May we contact this employer? ❑ Yes ❑ No	Hours Per Week	
Employer Phone		
Supervisor		
Reason for Leaving		

3.

Employer Name & Address	Dates Employed	Job Title/Duties
	Hourly Rate/Salary	
May we contact this employer? ❑ Yes ❑ No	Hours Per Week	
Employer Phone		
Supervisor		
Reason for Leaving		

4.

Employer Name & Address	Dates Employed	Job Title/Duties
	Hourly Rate/Salary	
May we contact this employer? ❑ Yes ❑ No	Hours Per Week	
Employer Phone		
Supervisor		
Reason for Leaving		

If you need additional space, continue on a separate sheet of paper.

Applicant's Statement

I certify that the information given on this application is true and complete to the best of my knowledge. I authorize investigation of all statements contained in this application, and understand that false or misleading information given in my application or interview(s) may result in discharge.

I understand and acknowledge that, unless otherwise defined by applicable law, any employment relationship with this organization is "at will," which means that I may resign at any time and the employer may discharge me at any time with or without cause. I further understand that this "at will" employment relationship may not be changed orally, by any written document, or by conduct, unless such change is specifically acknowledged in writing by an authorized executive of this organization.

_____   _____

Signature of Applicant   Date

EMPLOYMENT AGREEMENT

This employment agreement is entered into by and between _____ _____(the "Employee") and _____ _____ (the "Employer"), who agree as follows:

1. The Employer has hired the Employee to fill the following position:

    ❑ See attached description.

2. Term. The term of Employee's employment shall begin on _____. Employment pursuant to this agreement shall be "at will" and may be ended by the Employee or by the Employer at any time and for any reason. This is an agreement for employment that is:

    ❑ permanent, but "at will."

    ❑ temporary, but "at will," _____ _____.

3. Probation. It is understood that the first _____ days of employment shall be probationary only and that if the Employee's services are not satisfactory to the Employer, employment shall be terminated at the end of this probationary period.

4. Compensation and Benefits. The Employee's compensation and benefits during the term of this agreement shall be as stated in this paragraph, and may be adjusted from time to time by the Employer. Initially, the Employer shall pay the Employee:

    ❑ a salary in the amount of _____, payable _____.

    ❑ an hourly wage of $_____ , payable _____.

    ❑ a commission of _____% of _____.

    In addition to such commission, the Employee shall receive _____ _____.

    ❑ the following benefits: _____ _____.

    ❑ other:

5. Work Hours. The hours and schedule worked by the Employee may be adjusted from time to time by the Employer. Initially, the Employee shall work the following hours each week:

134

6. Additional Terms. The Employee also agrees to the terms of the attached:

❑ No other agreements are attached ❑ Confidentiality Agreement

❑ Agreement on Patents and Inventions ❑ Indemnification Agreement

❑ Other: _____

7. This agreement shall be governed by the laws of _____.

8. It is the Employer's intention to comply with all federal, state, and local laws that apply to the business, including, but not limited to, labor, equal opportunity, privacy, and sexual harassment laws. The Employee shall promptly report to the Employer any violations encountered in the business. The Employee shall at all times comply with any and all federal, state, and local laws.

9. The Employee shall not have the power to make any contracts or commitments on behalf of the Employer without the express written consent of the Employer.

10. In the event one party fails to insist upon performance of a part of this agreement, such failure shall not be construed as waiving those terms, and this entire agreement shall remain in full force.

11. In the event a dispute of any nature arises between the parties to this agreement, the parties agree to submit the dispute to binding arbitration under the rules of the American Arbitration Association. An award rendered by the arbitrator(s) shall be final and binding upon the parties and judgment on such award may be entered by either party in the highest court having jurisdiction. Each party specifically waives his or her right to bring the dispute before a court of law and stipulates that this agreement shall be a complete defense to any action instituted in any local, state, or federal court or before any administrative tribunal.

12. If any part of this agreement is adjudged invalid, illegal, or unenforceable, the remaining parts shall not be affected and shall remain in full force and effect.

13. This agreement shall be binding upon the parties, and upon their heirs, executors, personal representatives, administrators, and assigns. No person shall have a right or cause of action arising out of or resulting from this agreement except those who are parties to it and their successors in interest.

14. This instrument, including any attached agreements specified in paragraph 6 above, constitutes the entire agreement of the parties. No representations or promises have been made except those that are set out in this agreement. This agreement may not be modified except in writing signed by all the parties.

15. IN WITNESS WHEREOF the parties have signed this agreement under seal on _____.

Employer: Employee:

_____   _____

_____   _____

OMB No. 1615-0047; Expires 06/30/08

Department of Homeland Security
U.S. Citizenship and Immigration Services

**Form I-9, Employment
Eligibility Verification**

Please read instructions carefully before completing this form. The instructions must be available during completion of this form.

ANTI-DISCRIMINATION NOTICE: It is illegal to discriminate against work eligible individuals. Employers CANNOT specify which document(s) they will accept from an employee. The refusal to hire an individual because the documents have a future expiration date may also constitute illegal discrimination.

Section 1. Employee Information and Verification. To be completed and signed by employee at the time employment begins.

Print Name: Last	First	Middle Initial	Maiden Name

Address (Street Name and Number)	Apt. #	Date of Birth (month/day/year)

City	State	Zip Code	Social Security #

I am aware that federal law provides for imprisonment and/or fines for false statements or use of false documents in connection with the completion of this form.

I attest, under penalty of perjury, that I am (check one of the following):

☐ A citizen or national of the United States
☐ A lawful permanent resident (Alien #) A _____
☐ An alien authorized to work until _____
(Alien # or Admission #) _____

Employee's Signature	Date (month/day/year)

Preparer and/or Translator Certification. (To be completed and signed if Section 1 is prepared by a person other than the employee.) I attest, under penalty of perjury, that I have assisted in the completion of this form and that to the best of my knowledge the information is true and correct.

Preparer's/Translator's Signature	Print Name

Address (Street Name and Number, City, State, Zip Code)	Date (month/day/year)

Section 2. Employer Review and Verification. To be completed and signed by employer. Examine one document from List A OR examine one document from List B and one from List C, as listed on the reverse of this form, and record the title, number and expiration date, if any, of the document(s).

List A	OR	List B	AND	List C
Document title:				
Issuing authority:				
Document #:				
Expiration Date (if any):				
Document #:				
Expiration Date (if any):				

CERTIFICATION - I attest, under penalty of perjury, that I have examined the document(s) presented by the above-named employee, that the above-listed document(s) appear to be genuine and to relate to the employee named, that the employee began employment on *(month/day/year)* _____ **and that to the best of my knowledge the employee is eligible to work in the United States. (State employment agencies may omit the date the employee began employment.)**

Signature of Employer or Authorized Representative	Print Name	Title

Business or Organization Name and Address (Street Name and Number, City, State, Zip Code)	Date (month/day/year)

Section 3. Updating and Reverification. To be completed and signed by employer.

A. New Name (if applicable)	B. Date of Rehire (month/day/year) (if applicable)

C. If employee's previous grant of work authorization has expired, provide the information below for the document that establishes current employment eligibility.

Document Title:	Document #:	Expiration Date (if any):

I attest, under penalty of perjury, that to the best of my knowledge, this employee is eligible to work in the United States, and if the employee presented document(s), the document(s) I have examined appear to be genuine and to relate to the individual.

Signature of Employer or Authorized Representative	Date (month/day/year)

Form I-9 (Rev. 06/05/07) N

136

LISTS OF ACCEPTABLE DOCUMENTS

LIST A	LIST B	LIST C
Documents that Establish Both Identity and Employment Eligibility	**Documents that Establish Identity**	**Documents that Establish Employment Eligibility**
OR		AND
1. U.S. Passport (unexpired or expired)	1. Driver's license or ID card issued by a state or outlying possession of the United States provided it contains a photograph or information such as name, date of birth, gender, height, eye color and address	1. U.S. Social Security card issued by the Social Security Administration *(other than a card stating it is not valid for employment)*
2. Permanent Resident Card or Alien Registration Receipt Card (Form I-551)	2. ID card issued by federal, state or local government agencies or entities, provided it contains a photograph or information such as name, date of birth, gender, height, eye color and address	2. Certification of Birth Abroad issued by the Department of State *(Form FS-545 or Form DS-1350)*
3. An unexpired foreign passport with a temporary I-551 stamp	3. School ID card with a photograph	3. Original or certified copy of a birth certificate issued by a state, county, municipal authority or outlying possession of the United States bearing an official seal
4. An unexpired Employment Authorization Document that contains a photograph (Form I-766, I-688, I-688A, I-688B)	4. Voter's registration card	4. Native American tribal document
	5. U.S. Military card or draft record	5. U.S. Citizen ID Card *(Form I-197)*
5. An unexpired foreign passport with an unexpired Arrival-Departure Record, Form I-94, bearing the same name as the passport and containing an endorsement of the alien's nonimmigrant status, if that status authorizes the alien to work for the employer	6. Military dependent's ID card	6. ID Card for use of Resident Citizen in the United States *(Form I-179)*
	7. U.S. Coast Guard Merchant Mariner Card	
	8. Native American tribal document	7. Unexpired employment authorization document issued by DHS *(other than those listed under List A)*
	9. Driver's license issued by a Canadian government authority	
	For persons under age 18 who are unable to present a document listed above:	
	10. School record or report card	
	11. Clinic, doctor or hospital record	
	12. Day-care or nursery school record	

Illustrations of many of these documents appear in Part 8 of the Handbook for Employers (M-274)

Form I-9 (Rev. 06/05/07) N Page 2

OMB No. 1615-0047; Expires 06/30/08

Department of Homeland Security
U.S. Citizenship and Immigration Services

Form I-9, Employment Eligibility Verification

Instructions
Please read all instructions carefully before completing this form.

Anti-Discrimination Notice. It is illegal to discriminate against any individual (other than an alien not authorized to work in the U.S.) in hiring, discharging, or recruiting or referring for a fee because of that individual's national origin or citizenship status. It is illegal to discriminate against work eligible individuals. Employers **CANNOT** specify which document(s) they will accept from an employee. The refusal to hire an individual because the documents presented have a future expiration date may also constitute illegal discrimination.

What Is the Purpose of This Form?

The purpose of this form is to document that each new employee (both citizen and non-citizen) hired after November 6, 1986 is authorized to work in the United States.

When Should the Form I-9 Be Used?

All employees, citizens and noncitizens, hired after November 6, 1986 and working in the United States must complete a Form I-9.

Filling Out the Form I-9

Section 1, Employee: This part of the form must be completed at the time of hire, which is the actual beginning of employment. Providing the Social Security number is voluntary, except for employees hired by employers participating in the USCIS Electronic Employment Eligibility Verification Program (E-Verify). **The employer is responsible for ensuring that Section 1 is timely and properly completed.**

Preparer/Translator Certification. The Preparer/Translator Certification must be completed if **Section 1** is prepared by a person other than the employee. A preparer/translator may be used only when the employee is unable to complete **Section 1** on his/her own. However, the employee must still sign **Section 1** personally.

Section 2, Employer: For the purpose of completing this form, the term "employer" means all employers including those recruiters and referrers for a fee who are agricultural associations, agricultural employers or farm labor contractors.

Employers must complete **Section 2** by examining evidence of identity and employment eligibility within three (3) business days of the date employment begins. If employees are authorized to work, but are unable to present the required document(s) within three business days, they must present a receipt for the application of the document(s) within three business days and the actual document(s) within ninety (90) days. However, if employers hire individuals for a duration of less than three business days, **Section 2** must be completed at the time employment begins. **Employers must record:**

1. Document title;
2. Issuing authority;
3. Document number;
4. Expiration date, if any; and
5. The date employment begins.

Employers must sign and date the certification. Employees must present original documents. Employers may, but are not required to, photocopy the document(s) presented. These photocopies may only be used for the verification process and must be retained with the Form I-9. **However, employers are still responsible for completing and retaining the Form I-9.**

Section 3, Updating and Reverification: Employers must complete **Section 3** when updating and/or reverifying the Form I-9. Employers must reverify employment eligibility of their employees on or before the expiration date recorded in **Section 1.** Employers **CANNOT** specify which document(s) they will accept from an employee.

A. If an employee's name has changed at the time this form is being updated/reverified, complete Block A.

B. If an employee is rehired within three (3) years of the date this form was originally completed and the employee is still eligible to be employed on the same basis as previously indicated on this form (updating), complete Block B and the signature block.

C. If an employee is rehired within three (3) years of the date this form was originally completed and the employee's work authorization has expired **or** if a current employee's work authorization is about to expire (reverification), complete Block B and:

1. Examine any document that reflects that the employee is authorized to work in the U.S. (see List A **or** C);
2. Record the document title, document number and expiration date (if any) in Block C, and
3. Complete the signature block.

What Is the Filing Fee?

There is no associated filing fee for completing the Form I-9. This form is not filed with USCIS or any government agency. The Form I-9 must be retained by the employer and made available for inspection by U.S. Government officials as specified in the Privacy Act Notice below.

USCIS Forms and Information

To order USCIS forms, call our toll-free number at **1-800-870-3676**. Individuals can also get USCIS forms and information on immigration laws, regulations and procedures by telephoning our National Customer Service Center at **1-800-375-5283** or visiting our internet website at **www.uscis.gov**.

Photocopying and Retaining the Form I-9

A blank Form I-9 may be reproduced, provided both sides are copied. The Instructions must be available to all employees completing this form. Employers must retain completed Forms I-9 for three (3) years after the date of hire or one (1) year after the date employment ends, whichever is later.

The Form I-9 may be signed and retained electronically, as authorized in Department of Homeland Security regulations at 8 CFR § 274a.2.

Privacy Act Notice

The authority for collecting this information is the Immigration Reform and Control Act of 1986, Pub. L. 99-603 (8 USC 1324a).

This information is for employers to verify the eligibility of individuals for employment to preclude the unlawful hiring, or recruiting or referring for a fee, of aliens who are not authorized to work in the United States.

This information will be used by employers as a record of their basis for determining eligibility of an employee to work in the United States. The form will be kept by the employer and made available for inspection by officials of U.S. Immigration and Customs Enforcement, Department of Labor and Office of Special Counsel for Immigration Related Unfair Employment Practices.

Submission of the information required in this form is voluntary. However, an individual may not begin employment unless this form is completed, since employers are subject to civil or criminal penalties if they do not comply with the Immigration Reform and Control Act of 1986.

Paperwork Reduction Act

We try to create forms and instructions that are accurate, can be easily understood and which impose the least possible burden on you to provide us with information. Often this is difficult because some immigration laws are very complex. Accordingly, the reporting burden for this collection of information is computed as follows: **1)** learning about this form, and completing the form, 9 minutes; **2)** assembling and filing (recordkeeping) the form, 3 minutes, for an average of 12 minutes per response. If you have comments regarding the accuracy of this burden estimate, or suggestions for making this form simpler, you can write to: U.S. Citizenship and Immigration Services, Regulatory Management Division, 111 Massachusetts Avenue, N.W., 3rd Floor, Suite 3008, Washington, DC 20529. OMB No. 1615-0047.

CONFIDENTIALITY AGREEMENT

This agreement is made between _____ (the "Employee") and _____ (the "Employer"). The Employee agrees to the terms of this agreement:

☐ contemporaneously with and as part of the terms of the Employment Agreement by which the Employee is being hired by the Employer, which Employment Agreement is incorporated by reference.

☐ in consideration of the Employee's continued employment by the Employer and additional consideration consisting of _____, which the Employee acknowledges is sufficient consideration paid by the Employer over and above the consideration due to the Employee pursuant to his or her usual terms of employment.

1. The Employee acknowledges that, in the course of employment by the Employer, the Employee has, and may in the future, come into the possession of certain confidential information belonging to the Employer, including, but not limited to, trade secrets, customer lists, supplier lists and prices, pricing schedules, methods, processes, or marketing plans.

2. The Employee hereby covenants and agrees that he or she will at no time, during or after the term of employment, use for his or her own benefit or the benefit of others, or disclose or divulge to others, any such confidential information.

3. Upon termination of employment, the Employee will return to the Employer, retaining no copies, all documents relating to the Employer's business including, but not limited to, reports, manuals, drawings, diagrams, blueprints, correspondence, customer lists, computer programs, and all other materials and all copies of such materials, obtained by the Employee during employment.

4. Violation of this agreement by the Employee will entitle the Employer to an injunction to prevent such competition or disclosure (posting of any bond by the Employer is hereby waived), and will entitle the Employer to other legal remedies, including attorney's fees and costs.

5. This agreement shall be governed by the laws of _____.

6. If any part of this agreement is adjudged invalid, illegal, or unenforceable, the remaining parts shall not be affected and shall remain in full force and effect.

7. This agreement shall be binding upon the parties, and upon their heirs, executors, personal representatives, administrators, and assigns. No person shall have a right or cause of action arising out of or resulting from this agreement except those who are parties to it and their successors in interest.

8. This instrument, including any attached exhibits and addenda, constitutes the entire agreement of the parties. No representations or promises have been made except those that are set out in this agreement. This agreement may not be modified except in writing signed by all the parties.

IN WITNESS WHEREOF the parties have signed this agreement under seal on
_____.

Employer: Employee:

_____   _____

_____   _____

EMPLOYEE'S AGREEMENT ON PATENTS AND INVENTIONS

This agreement is made between _____
(the "Employee") and _____ (the
"Employer"). The Employee agrees to the terms of this agreement:

- ❑ contemporaneously with and as part of the terms of the Employment Agreement by which the Employee is being hired by the Employer, which Employment Agreement is incorporated by reference.

- ❑ in consideration of the Employee's continued employment by the Employer and additional consideration consisting of _____, which the Employee acknowledges is sufficient consideration paid by the Employer over and above the consideration due to the Employee pursuant to his or her usual terms of employment.

1. During the term of the Employee's employment and for a period of _____ months thereafter, the Employee will promptly and completely disclose and assign to the Employer every invention, product, process, mechanism, or design that the Employee may invent, create, develop, or discover that in any way relates to, or may be suggested by, the Employer's business or the Employee's employment duties. Such disclosure or assignment shall be made free of any obligation by the Employer to the Employee and without the necessity of any further request by the Employer.

2. The Employee will, at the Employer's expense, cooperate with the Employer in applying for and securing in the name of the Employer patents with respect to the matters required to be disclosed pursuant to this agreement in each country where the Employer wishes to secure such patents. Without limiting the foregoing, the Employee will promptly execute all proper documents presented to him or her for signature by the Employer in connection with the securing of such patents and the transfer of such patents to the Employer and will give such true information and testimony, under oath if so requested, as the Employer may reasonably require in connection with such matters.

3. The following is a complete list of all inventions, applications for patent, and patents in which the Employee holds an interest, and which are not subject to this agreement:

4. This agreement shall be governed by the laws of _____.

5. If any part of this agreement is adjudged invalid, illegal, or unenforceable, the remaining parts shall not be affected and shall remain in full force and effect.

6. This agreement shall be binding upon the parties, and upon their heirs, executors, personal representatives, administrators, and assigns. No person shall have a right or cause of action arising out of or resulting from this agreement except those who are parties to it and their successors in interest.

7. This instrument, including any attached exhibits and addenda, constitutes the entire agreement of the parties. No representations or promises have been made except those that are set out in this agreement. This agreement may not be modified except in writing signed by all the parties.

IN WITNESS WHEREOF the parties have signed this agreement under seal on

_____.

Employer: Employee:

_____   _____

_____   _____

NON-COMPETITION AGREEMENT

This agreement is made between _____
(the "Employee") and _____ (the
"Employer"). The Employee agrees to the terms of this agreement:

- ❏ contemporaneously with and as part of the terms of the Employment Agreement by which the Employee is being hired by the Employer, which Employment Agreement is incorporated by reference.

- ❏ in consideration of the Employee's continued employment by the Employer and additional consideration consisting of _____, which the Employee acknowledges is sufficient consideration paid by the Employer over and above the consideration due to the Employee pursuant to his or her usual terms of employment.

1. The Employee agrees that he or she will not compete, directly or indirectly, as a business owner, partner, corporation, employee, agent, or otherwise with the business of the Employer or any of the Employer's successors or assigns.

2. "Not compete," as used herein, shall mean that the Employee, directly or indirectly, as an owner, partner, officer, director, stockholder, employee, consultant, agent, or otherwise (except as a passive investment stockholder in a publicly owned corporation), shall not engage in any business or activity described as: _____
_____,

3. This agreement shall apply to such business or activity within the following geographical area: _____,
and shall remain in full force and effect for a period of _____.

4. In the event of any breach of this agreement by the Employee, the Employer shall be entitled to injunctive relief without posting any bond, in addition to any other legal rights and remedies.

5. This agreement shall be governed by the laws of _____.

6. If any part of this agreement is adjudged invalid, illegal, or unenforceable, the remaining parts shall not be affected and shall remain in full force and effect, and any such time period and geographical limitations stated in this agreement shall be amended to allow enforcement to the nearest extent permitted by law.

7. This agreement shall be binding upon the parties, and upon their heirs, executors, personal representatives, administrators, and assigns. No person shall have a right or cause of action arising out of or resulting from this agreement except those who are parties to it and their successors in interest.

8. This instrument, including any attached exhibits and addenda, constitutes the entire agreement of the parties. No representations or promises have been made except those that are set out in this agreement. This agreement may not be modified except in writing signed by all the parties.

IN WITNESS WHEREOF the parties have signed this agreement under seal on

_____.

Employer: Employee:

_____   _____

_____   _____

APPOINTMENT OF INDEPENDENT SALES REPRESENTATIVE

This agreement is entered into by and between _____ (the "Agent") and _____ (the "Company"). It is agreed by the Agent and the Company as follows:

1. The Company has appointed the Agent as its representative for the sale of _____ in the following territory: _____. The territory may be changed from time to time upon agreement by the Company and the Agent. The Agent agrees to use his or her best efforts in the sale of such in the territory assigned.

2. The term of Agent's appointment shall begin on _____, and may be ended by the Agent or by the Company at any time and for any reason.

3. All sales made by the Agent shall be at prices and terms set by the Company, and no sales contracts shall be valid until accepted by a duly authorized officer of the Company.

4. The Agent's compensation and benefits during the term of this agreement shall be as stated in this paragraph, and may be adjusted from time to time by the Company. The Company shall pay the Agent a commission of _____% based on the net selling price of the goods actually received by the Company. In the event part or all of the purchase price is refunded to the purchaser for any reason, the Agent's commission based on such amounts refunded shall be returned by the Agent to the Company or deducted by the Company from the Agent's future commissions. The Company shall not be liable to the Agent for commissions on orders unfilled by the Company for any reason. In addition to the commissions provided for in this agreement, the Agent shall receive

_____

_____.

5. The Company shall reimburse the Agent for expenses according to a schedule published from time to time by the Company.

6. The parties agree that no employer-employee relationship is created by this agreement, but the relationship of the Agent to the Company shall be that of an independent contractor.

7. This agreement shall be governed by the laws of _____. If any part of this agreement is adjudged invalid, illegal, or unenforceable, the remaining parts shall not be affected and shall remain in full force and effect. This agreement shall be binding upon the parties, and upon their heirs, executors, personal representatives, administrators, and assigns. No person shall have a right or cause of action arising out of or resulting from this agreement except those who are parties to it and their successors in interest.

8. This instrument, including any attached exhibits and addenda, constitutes the entire agreement of the parties. No representations or promises have been made except those that are set out in this agreement. This agreement may not be modified except in writing signed by all the parties.

IN WITNESS WHEREOF the parties have signed this agreement under seal on
_____.

Company: Agent:

_____   _____

_____   _____

WORK MADE-FOR-HIRE AGREEMENT

This Agreement is made this _____ day of _____, _____, between _____ as Owner, and _____as Author/Artist.

WHEREAS the Owner wishes to commission a Work called _____ _____ and;

WHEREAS the Author/Artist has represented that he/she can create said work according to the specifications provided by the Owner;

It is agreed between the parties hereto that in consideration of the sum of $_____, to be paid by the Owner to the Author/Artist within thirty days of satisfactory completion of the work, the Author/Artist shall create the Work as specified. Upon payment, the Owner shall acquire all rights to the commissioned Work, including copyright.

The Author/Artist warrants that the Work will be original and will not infringe or plagiarize any other work; will not libel any person or invade any person's right to privacy; and, will not contain any unlawful materials. The Author/Artist shall indemnify and save the Owner harmless from any loss or liability due to any breach of these warranties, including reasonable attorney's fees.

The Author/Artist shall be responsible for all costs in creation of the Work unless otherwise agreed to in writing by the Owner.

This agreement shall be governed by the laws of _____.

If any part of this agreement is adjudged invalid, illegal, or unenforceable, the remaining parts shall not be affected and shall remain in full force and effect.

This agreement shall be binding upon the parties, and upon their heirs, executors, personal representatives, administrators, and assigns. No person shall have a right or cause of action arising out of or resulting from this agreement except those who are parties to it and their successors in interest.

This instrument, including any attached exhibits and addenda, constitutes the entire agreement of the parties. No representations or promises have been made except those that are set out in this agreement. This agreement may not be modified except in writing signed by all the parties.

IN WITNESS WHEREOF the parties have signed this agreement under seal on _____.

Owner: Author/Artist:

_____   _____

_____   _____

This page intentionally blank.

INDEPENDENT CONTRACTOR AGREEMENT

This indemnification agreement is entered into by and between _____ _____ (the "Company") and _____ _____ (the "Contractor"). It is agreed by the parties as follows:

1. The Contractor shall supply all the labor and materials to perform the following work for the Company as an independent contractor:

❑ The attached plans and specifications are to be followed and are hereby made a part of this Agreement.

2. The Contractor agrees to the following completion dates for portions of the work and final completion of the work:

Description of Work   Completion Date

3. The Contractor shall perform the work in a workmanlike manner, according to standard industry practices, unless other standards or requirements are set forth in any attached plans and specifications.

4. The Company shall pay the Contractor the sum of $_____, in full payment for the work as set forth in this Agreement, to be paid as follows:

5. Any additional work or services shall be agreed to in writing, signed by both parties.

6. The Contractor shall obtain and maintain any licenses or permits necessary for the work to be performed. The Contractor shall obtain and maintain any required

insurance, including but not limited to workers' compensation insurance, to cover the Contractor's employees and agents.

7. The Contractor shall be responsible for the payment of any sub-contractors and shall obtain lien releases from sub-contractors as may be necessary. The Contractor agrees to indemnify and hold harmless the Company from any claims or liability arising out of the work performed by the Contractor under this Agreement.

8. Time is of the essence of this Agreement.

9. This instrument, including any attached exhibits and addenda, constitutes the entire agreement of the parties. No representations or promises have been made except those that are set out in this agreement. This agreement may not be modified except in writing signed by all the parties.

10. This agreement shall be governed by the laws of _____.

11. If any part of this agreement is adjudged invalid, illegal, or unenforceable, the remaining parts shall not be affected and shall remain in full force and effect.

12. This agreement shall be binding upon the parties, and upon their heirs, executors, personal representatives, administrators, and assigns. No person shall have a right or cause of action arising out of or resulting from this agreement except those who are parties to it and their successors in interest.

13. This instrument, including any attached exhibits and addenda, constitutes the entire agreement of the parties. No representations or promises have been made except those that are set out in this agreement. This agreement may not be modified except in writing signed by all the parties.

IN WITNESS WHEREOF the parties have signed this agreement under seal on _____.

Company: Contractor:

_____   _____

_____   _____

PARTNERSHIP AGREEMENT

This Partnership Agreement is entered into this _____ day of _____,
_____, by and between the following partners: _____
_____,
who agree as follows:

1. **Name of Partnership.** The name of the partnership shall be: _____
    _____.
    The name under which the partnership shall conduct business shall be: _____
    _____.

2. **Principal Place of Business.** The partnership's principal place of business shall
    be: _____.

3. **Purpose of Partnership.** The purposes of the partnership are: _____
    _____.
    In addition to the specific purposes set forth above, the purpose of the partnership
    is also to conduct any lawful business in which the partners, from time to time,
    may agree to become engaged.

4. **Term of Partnership.** The partnership shall become effective as of the date of this
    agreement, and shall continue until it is dissolved by all the partners, or until a
    partner leaves for any reason including incapacity or death, or until otherwise dis-
    solved by law.

5. **Contributions of Partners.** Each partner shall make an initial cash contribu-
    tion to the partnership in the amount of $_____.

6. **Profits and Losses/Ownership Interests.** The partners shall share equally in
    the profits and losses of the partnership.

7. **Voting Rights.** All partnership decisions must be made by the unanimous agree-
    ment of the partners. All matters not referred to in this agreement shall be deter-
    mined according to this paragraph.

8. **Transfer of a Partnership Interest.**

    A. **Option of Partnership to Purchase/Right of First Refusal.** In the event
        any partner leaves the partnership; for whatever reason, including voluntary
        withdrawal or retirement, incapacity, or death; the remaining partners shall
        have the option to purchase said partner's interest from said partner or his or

her estate. In the event any partner receives, and is willing to accept, an offer from a person who is not a partner to purchase all his or her interest in the partnership, he or she shall notify the other partners of the identity of the proposed buyer, the amount and terms of the offer, and of his or her willingness to accept the offer. The other partners shall then have the option, within thirty days after notice is given, to purchase that partner's interest in the partnership name on the same terms as those of the offer of the person who is not a partner, to put the business up for sale, or to dissolve the partnership.

B. **Valuation of Partnership.** In the event the remaining partners exercise the right to purchase the other's interest as provided above, the value of the partnership shall be the net worth of the partnership as of the date of such purchase. Net worth shall be determined by the market value of the following assets: all of the partnership's real and personal property, liquid assets, accounts receivable, earned but unbilled fees, and money earned for work in progress; less the total amount of all debts owed by the partnership.

C. **Payment Upon Buy-Out.** In the event the remaining partners exercise the right to purchase the other's interest as provided above, the remaining partners shall pay the departing partner for his or her interest by way of a promissory note of the partnership, dated as of the date of purchase, which shall mature in not more than _____ years, and shall bear interest at the rate of _____% per annum. The first payment shall be made _____ days after the date of the promissory note.

9. **Governing Law.** This agreement shall be governed by the laws of _____.

10. **Severability.** If any part of this agreement is adjudged invalid, illegal, or unenforceable, the remaining parts shall not be affected and shall remain in full force and effect.

11. **Binding Agreement/No Other Beneficiary.** This agreement shall be binding upon the parties, and upon their heirs, executors, personal representatives, administrators, and assigns. No person shall have a right or cause of action arising or resulting from this agreement except those who are parties to it and their successors in interest.

12. **Entire Agreement.** This instrument, including any attached exhibits, constitutes the entire agreement of the parties. No representations or promises have been made except those that are set out in this agreement. This agreement may not be modified except in writing signed by the parties.

13. **Paragraph Headings.** The headings of the paragraphs contained in this agreement are for convenience only, and are not to be considered a part of this agreement or used in determining its content or context.

_____   _____
Signature   Signature

_____   _____
Signature   Signature

_____   _____
Signature   Signature

This page intentionally blank.

LIMITED POWER OF ATTORNEY

_____ (the "Grantor") hereby grants to _____ (the "Agent") a limited power of attorney. As the Grantor's attorney in fact, the Agent shall have full power and authority to undertake and perform the following on behalf of the Grantor:

By accepting this grant, the Agent agrees to act in a fiduciary capacity consistent with the reasonable best interests of the Grantor. This power of attorney may be revoked by the Grantor at any time; however, any person dealing with the Agent as attorney in fact may rely on this appointment until receipt of actual notice of termination.

IN WITNESS WHEREOF, the undersigned grantor has executed this power of attorney under seal as of the _____ day of _____, 20_____.

Witness/Attest:_____   _____(Seal)

                  ,   , Grantor

STATE OF
COUNTY OF

I certify that _____, who ❏ is personally known to me to be the person whose name is subscribed to the foregoing instrument ❏ produced _____ as identification, personally appeared before me on _____, and ❏ acknowledged the execution of the foregoing instrument ❏ acknowledged that (s)he is (Assistant) Secretary of _____ and that by authority duly given and as the act of the corporation, the foregoing instrument was signed in its name by its (Vice) President, sealed with its corporate seal, and attested by him/her as its (Assistant) Secretary.

_____

Notary Public, State of
Notary's commission expires:

I hereby accept the foregoing appointment as attorney in fact on _____.

_____

Attorney in Fact

This page intentionally blank.

POWER OF ATTORNEY

_____ (the "Grantor") hereby grants to _____(the "Agent") a general power of attorney. As the Grantor's attorney in fact, the Agent shall have full power and authority to undertake any and all acts that may be lawfully undertaken on behalf of the grantor including, but not limited to, the right to buy, sell, lease, mortgage, assign, rent, or otherwise dispose of any real or personal property belonging to the Grantor; to execute, accept, undertake, and perform contracts in the name of the Grantor; to deposit, endorse, or withdraw funds to or from any bank depository of the Grantor; to initiate, defend, or settle legal actions on behalf of the Grantor; and, to retain any accountant, attorney, or other advisor deemed by the Agent to be necessary to protect the interests of the Grantor in relation to such powers.

By accepting this grant, the Agent agrees to act in a fiduciary capacity consistent with the reasonable best interests of the Grantor. This power of attorney may be revoked by the Grantor at any time; however, any person dealing with the Agent as attorney in fact may rely on this appointment until receipt of actual notice of termination.

IN WITNESS WHEREOF, the undersigned grantor has executed this power of attorney under seal as of the _____ day of _____, 20_____.

Witness/Attest:_____   _____(Seal)
                      ,   , Grantor

STATE OF
COUNTY OF

I certify that _____, who ❑ is personally known to me to be the person whose name is subscribed to the foregoing instrument ❑ produced _____ as identification, personally appeared before me on _____, and ❑ acknowledged the execution of the foregoing instrument ❑ acknowledged that (s)he is (Assistant) Secretary of _____ and that by authority duly given and as the act of the corporation, the foregoing instrument was signed in its name by its (Vice) President, sealed with its corporate seal, and attested by him/her as its (Assistant) Secretary.

_____
Notary Public, State of
Notary's commission expires:

I hereby accept the foregoing appointment as attorney in fact on _____.

_____
                                          Attorney in Fact

This page intentionally blank.

REVOCATION OF POWER OF ATTORNEY

_____ (the "Grantor") hereby revokes the Power of Attorney dated _____, appointing _____ _____ as the Agent and attorney in fact to act on behalf of the Grantor.

This revocation shall be effective on the ____ day of _____, 20 ___ .

_____ (Signature of Grantor)

_____ (Typed or printed name of Grantor)

_____ (Address)

_____

_____

I hereby acknowledge receipt of the foregoing revocation of power of attorney on the ____ day of _____, 20 ___ .

_____

Attorney in Fact

This page intentionally blank.

CREDIT APPLICATION

☐ Individual

☐ Business: ☐ Corporation   ☐ Partnership   ☐ Other: _____

Annual gross sales $_____   Annual net profit $_____   Net value $_____

Name:	Address:
Social Security Number:	
Spouse's Name:	
Spouse's Social Security Number:	Telephone:
Previous Address(es):	
Employer (Name, Address, and Phone):	Previous Employer:
Position:	Position:
Annual Income:	Annual Income:
Spouse's Employer (Name, Address, and Phone):	Spouse's Previous Employer:
Position:	Position:
Annual Income:	Annual Income:
Other Income:	
Bank and Credit References:	
Trade References:	
If a business, state names and addresses of owners, partners, or officers:	

This page intentionally blank.

REQUEST FOR CREDIT REFERENCE INFORMATION

To: _____

     _____

     _____

Re: Credit reference for _____ (Borrower)

Dear Sir or Madam:

The Borrower named above has submitted a credit application to the undersigned and has named your institution as a credit reference. Attached to this letter is a copy of the Borrower's application naming you as a reference and authorizing you to release credit information to us.

Please provide the following information:

Please contact the undersigned if you have questions regarding this request.

Sincerely,

_____ (Name of contact person)

_____ (Title)

_____ (Company and address)

_____

_____

This page intentionally blank.

PROMISSORY NOTE

$_____   Date:_____

_____ hereby
promises to pay to the order of _____
_____ the sum of $_____,
with interest thereon from the date of this note to the date of payment at the rate of
interest per annum as set forth below:

This note is due payable in full on _____, if not paid sooner. The principal and interest shall be payable when due at _____
_____ or at a place
of which the undersigned may be notified in writing by the holder of this note.

This note is not assumable without the written consent of the lender. This note
may be paid in whole or in part at any time prior without penalty. The borrower waives
demand, presentment, protest, and notice. This note shall be fully payable upon
demand of any holder in the event the undersigned shall default on the terms of this
note or any agreement securing the payment of this note. In the event of default, the
undersigned agrees to pay all costs of collection including reasonable attorney's fees.

IN WITNESS WHEREOF, the undersigned has executed this note under seal as of
the date stated above (if the undersigned is a corporation, this note has been executed
under seal and by authority of its board of directors).

_____

_____

This page intentionally blank.

ASSIGNMENT OF MORTGAGE

For and in consideration of _____,
the receipt of which is hereby acknowledged, _____
_____ hereby assigns, grants, and transfers to _____,
_____ that certain mortgage dated _____,
executed by _____,
and recorded at _____
_____, together
with the note described therein and the money together with the interest due thereon.

IN WITNESS WHEREOF, the undersigned has executed this assignment on the
_____ day of _____, _____.

Witnessed/Attested by: _____

_____

_____

STATE OF   )
COUNTY OF   )

I certify that _____, who ❑ is personally known to
me to be the person whose name is subscribed to the foregoing instrument ❑ produced
_____ as identification, personally appeared before me on
_____, and ❑ acknowledged the execution of the foregoing
instrument ❑ acknowledged that (s)he is (Assistant) Secretary of _____
_____ and that by authority duly given
and as the act of the corporation, the foregoing instrument was signed in its name by
its (Vice) President, sealed with its corporate seal, and attested by him/her as its
(Assistant) Secretary.

_____

Notary Public, State of

My commission expires:

This page intentionally blank.

SATISFACTION OF MORTGAGE

For value received, _____,
the holder(s) of that certain mortgage dated _____, executed by _____,
and recorded at _____
_____,
hereby acknowledge(s) full payment, satisfaction, and discharge of said mortgage.

IN WITNESS WHEREOF, the undersigned has executed this satisfaction of mortgage on the _____ day of _____, _____.

Witnessed/Attested by: _____

_____

_____

STATE OF   )
COUNTY OF   )

I certify that _____, who ❑ is personally known to
me to be the person whose name is subscribed to the foregoing instrument ❑ produced
_____ as identification, personally appeared before
me on _____, and ❑ acknowledged the execution of the foregoing
instrument ❑ acknowledged that (s)he is (Assistant) Secretary of _____
_____ and that by authority duly given
and as the act of the corporation, the foregoing instrument was signed in its name by
its (Vice) President, sealed with its corporate seal, and attested by him/her as its
(Assistant) Secretary.

_____
Notary Public, State of

My commission expires:

This page intentionally blank.

SECURITY AGREEMENT

In exchange for valuable consideration, the receipt and sufficiency of which is hereby acknowledged by the undersigned, _____ (the "Debtor") hereby grants to _____ (the "Creditor") a security interest in _____ to secure the payment and performance of the Debtor's obligations described as follows (the "Obligations"):

Upon any default by the Debtor in the performance of any of the Obligations, the Creditor may declare all obligations of the Debtor immediately due and payable and shall have the remedies of a secured party under the Uniform Commercial Code enacted in the state the laws of which govern the terms of this agreement.

This agreement is executed by the Debtor under seal on _____.

_____

_____

This page intentionally blank.

DISCHARGE OF SECURITY INTEREST

The undersigned, _____
(the "Creditor") hereby discharges and releases _____
_____ (the "Debtor") from the Security
Agreement dated _____, _____, covering the following property:

Any claims or obligations that are not specifically stated in this instrument are not released or discharged by this instrument. No assignment of any claim or obligation stated in this instrument has been made by the Creditor. The Creditor agrees to execute a Release of UCC Financing Statement, if requested by the Debtor.

This agreement is executed by the Creditor under seal on _____.

_____

_____

This page intentionally blank.

SALES AGREEMENT

This agreement is made by and between _____
_____ (the "Seller") and _____
_____, (the Buyer), who agree as follows:

1. The Seller agrees to sell, and the Buyer agrees to buy:

2. In exchange for the Property, the Buyer agrees to pay to the Seller the sum of $_____, payable according to the terms of a promissory note, a copy of which is attached to this agreement and incorporated into this agreement by reference (the "Note").

3. The Seller retains a security interest in the Property to secure payment and performance of the Buyer's obligations under this agreement and the Note. Upon any default by the Buyer in the performance of any such obligations, the Seller may declare all obligations immediately due and payable and shall have the remedies of a secured party under the Uniform Commercial Code enacted in the state the laws of which govern the terms of this agreement.

4. This agreement shall be governed by the laws of _____.

5. If any part of this agreement is adjudged invalid, illegal, or unenforceable, the remaining parts shall not be affected and shall remain in full force and effect.

6. This agreement shall be binding upon the parties, and upon their heirs, executors, personal representatives, administrators, and assigns. No person shall have a right or cause of action arising out of or resulting from this agreement except those who are parties to it and their successors in interest.

7. This instrument, including any attached exhibits and addenda, constitutes the entire agreement of the parties. No representations or promises have been made except those that are set out in this agreement. This agreement may not be modified except in writing signed by all the parties.

IN WITNESS WHEREOF the parties have signed this agreement under seal on
_____.

Seller: Buyer:

_____   _____

_____   _____

This page intentionally blank.

CONSIGNMENT SALES AGREEMENT

This agreement is made by and between _____ (the Consignor") and _____ (the "Consignee").

1. The Consignor and Consignee acknowledge and agree that the Consignor has provided the goods described below to Consignee for sale on a consignment basis, for the prices indicated, under the terms and conditions of this agreement:

2. The Consignee agrees to use its best efforts to sell the goods, for cash, for the benefit of the Consignor and to account to the Consignor for such sales within _____, delivering the sale proceeds to the Consignor, less commission, at the time of the accounting.

3. The Consignee agrees to accept as its commission, in full payment for its performance under this agreement, an amount equal to _____% of the gross sales price of the goods exclusive of any sales taxes.

4. Any goods the Consignee is unable to sell may be returned to the Consignor at the expense of the Consignee. The Consignor may reclaim unsold goods at any time.

5. At the request of the Consignor, the Consignee agrees to execute financing statements perfecting the Consignor's claim of ownership of the goods.

6. This agreement shall be governed by the laws of _____.

7. If any part of this agreement is adjudged invalid, illegal, or unenforceable, the remaining parts shall not be affected and shall remain in full force and effect.

8. This agreement shall be binding upon the parties, and upon their heirs, executors, personal representatives, administrators, and assigns. No person shall have a right or cause of action arising out of or resulting from this agreement except those who are parties to it and their successors in interest.

9. This instrument, including any attached exhibits and addenda, constitutes the entire agreement of the parties. No representations or promises have been made except those that are set out in this agreement. This agreement may not be modified except in writing signed by all the parties.

IN WITNESS WHEREOF the parties have signed this agreement under seal on _____.

Consignor: Consignee:

_____   _____

_____   _____

This page intentionally blank.

BILL OF SALE

For valuable consideration, the receipt and sufficiency of which is hereby acknowledged, the undersigned hereby sells and transfers to _____ the following:

The undersigned warrants and represents that it has good title to and full authority to sell and transfer the same and that the property is sold and transferred free and clear of all liens, claims, and encumbrances except:

Executed under seal on _____.

_____

BILL OF SALE

For valuable consideration, the receipt and sufficiency of which is hereby acknowledged, the undersigned hereby sells and transfers to _____ the following:

The undersigned warrants and represents that it has good title to and full authority to sell and transfer the same and that the property is sold and transferred free and clear of all liens, claims, and encumbrances except:

The undersigned warrants that, subject to the exceptions stated above, it will indemnify the Buyer, and defend title to the property, against the adverse claims of all persons.

Executed under seal on _____.

_____

This page intentionally blank.

NOTICE OF REJECTION OF NON-CONFORMING GOODS

Date: _____

To:

Re: Purchase Order No._____

We hereby reject the delivery of the goods specified in the above-mentioned purchase order. We received delivery on _____, _____, however, the goods do not conform to the specifications and requirements of our purchase order for the following reasons:

We paid for the goods with check number _____, dated _____, in the sum of $_____. In the event you have not yet cashed this check, please return the check to us. If the check has been cashed, we hereby demand a refund of this amount. If we do not receive a refund within _____ days of the date of this Notice, we will take legal action for the refund.

Please notify us of your desires regarding the disposition of the goods at your expense. If we do not receive instructions within _____ days of the date of this Notice, we will not accept any responsibility for storage.

Please be advised that we reserve all rights available to us under the Uniform Commercial Code and any other applicable law.

_____

This page intentionally blank.

NOTICE OF CONDITIONAL ACCEPTANCE OF NON-CONFORMING GOODS

Date: _____

To:

Re: Purchase Order No._____

You are hereby notified that the goods delivered to us on _____, pursuant to the above-mentioned purchase order, do not conform to the specifications and requirements of our purchase order for the following reasons:

Although we are under no obligation to accept such non-conforming goods, we are willing to accept them on the following condition(s):

If you do not notify us in writing that you are accepting these terms within _____ days of the date of this Notice, we will reject the goods and they will be returned to you at your expense.

Please be advised that we reserve all rights available to us under the Uniform Commercial Code and any other applicable law.

_____

This page intentionally blank.

DEMAND FOR PAYMENT

Date: _____

To:

    Your account is delinquent in the amount of $_____.

    Please be advised that in the event we do not receive payment in full within _____ days of the date of this notice, we will initiate collection proceedings against you without further notice. If such proceedings are initiated, you will also be responsible for pre-judgment interest, attorney's fees, court costs, and any and all other costs of collection. Collection proceedings may also adversely affect your credit rating.

    If full payment has already been sent, please disregard this notice.

    Please contact the undersigned if you have any questions.

                                              _____

This page intentionally blank.

FINAL DEMAND FOR PAYMENT

Date: _____

To:

Your account is delinquent in the amount of $ _____.

By letter(s) dated _____ you were reminded that your account is overdue and demanding immediate payment. As of the date of this notice, your account remains unpaid in the amount shown above. If payment in full is not received within ___ days of the date of this notice, we will initiate collection proceedings against you. If such proceedings are initiated, you will also be responsible for pre-judgment interest, attorney's fees, court costs, and any and all other costs of collection to the full extent allowed by law. Failure to pay your account in full may adversely affect your credit rating.

If full payment has already been sent, please disregard this notice.

Please contact the undersigned if you have any questions.

THIS IS YOUR FINAL NOTICE. TO AVOID THE ADVERSE CONSEQUENCES DESCRIBED ABOVE, GIVE THIS MATTER YOUR IMMEDIATE ATTENTION!

Sincerely,

_____

This page intentionally blank.

NOTICE OF ASSIGNMENT OF ACCOUNT FOR COLLECTION

Date: _____

To:

    Please be advised that your delinquent account has been assigned for collection to the following collection agent: _____
_____.
The amount assigned is based upon the following amount(s):

    Please contact the above-mentioned collection agent regarding this notice and all future payments on this account.

_____

This page intentionally blank.

BAD CHECK NOTICE

Date: _____

To:

Dear Sir or Madam:

A check drawn by you has been returned to us unpaid because of insufficient funds. The check is described below:

Check number: _____

Date of check: _____

The check was drawn of the following bank: _____

The check is made payable to: _____

The check is signed by: _____

We request that, no later than _____ (date), you replace this check with cash payment in the amount of $_____ plus a return check fee of $_____ .

Please send your payment in the total amount of $_____ to the undersigned at the address given below. We appreciate your prompt attention to this matter. Please contact us at ( ) ___ - _____ if you have any questions.

Sincerely,

_____

_____

_____

_____

This page intentionally blank.

CASH RECEIPT

The undersigned hereby certifies and acknowledges that on _____,
(s)he received from _____
❑ the cash sum of $_____   ❑ a check in the amount of $_____
in payment for:

_____

RECEIPT FOR PERSONAL PROPERTY

The undersigned hereby certifies and acknowledges that on _____,
(s)he received from _____
the following personal property:

The purpose for which such items were received was:

_____

This page intentionally blank.

CONTRACT FOR COMPANY'S SERVICES

This agreement is made between _____
(the "Company") and _____
(the "Customer"). The Company and the Customer agree as follows:

1. The Company will provide the following services to the Customer under the terms and conditions of this agreement:

2. The Company agrees to perform such services diligently, using its best efforts and providing competent personnel and adequate time to complete the work to professional standards of high quality. The Company may perform such services at the times and locations as may be agreed by the parties.

3. As payment for the completed services described above, and in addition to the release provided in paragraph 5 below, the Customer shall pay to the Company the sum of $_____, payable in the following manner:

4. The services to be provided by the Company pursuant to this agreement shall begin not later than _____, and shall be completed not later than _____.

5. DISCLAIMER OF LIABILITY AND RELEASE BY CUSTOMER—READ CAREFULLY: The Company has informed the Customer, and the Customer acknowledges having been informed, that the performance of the services described above involves certain inherent risks and dangers including, but not limited to, the following:

THE COMPANY DISCLAIMS ALL LIABILITY FOR DAMAGES AND INJURIES THAT MAY RESULT FROM ALL RISKS REFERRED TO IN THIS PARAGRAPH, and the Customer, having been so informed, in further consideration of the Company's willingness to provide such services, hereby releases, discharges, and acquits the Company, and its employees, agents, successors, and assigns, from any and all claims, actions, suits, or liabilities that may arise as a result of or in connection with the performance of the services not resulting directly and wholly from the negligence of the Company, its agents, and its employees.

6. The parties agree that no employer-employee relationship is created by this agreement, but that the relationship of the Company to the Customer shall be that of an independent contractor.

7. This agreement shall be governed by the laws of _____.

8. If any part of this agreement is adjudged invalid, illegal, or unenforceable, the remaining parts shall not be affected and shall remain in full force and effect.

9. This agreement shall be binding upon the parties, and upon their heirs, executors, personal representatives, administrators, and assigns. No person shall have a right or cause of action arising out of or resulting from this agreement except those who are parties to it and their successors in interest.

10. This instrument, including any attached exhibits and addenda, constitutes the entire agreement of the parties. No representations or promises have been made except those that are set out in this agreement. This agreement may not be modified except in writing signed by all the parties.

IN WITNESS WHEREOF the parties have signed this agreement under seal on _____.

_____   _____

_____   _____

COMPLAINT REGARDING DEFECTIVE SERVICE

Date: _____

TO:

Dear Sir or Madam:

The purpose of this letter is to register a complaint about a service I received from you. The service I received is described below:

The service you provided was defective or inadequate in the following way:

I have previously complained about this problem to the person and on the date indicated below:

As of the date of this letter, no action has been taken to resolve this complaint. On the dates listed below, I have paid the following amount(s) toward the cost of this service:

I would appreciate your assistance in resolving this matter. Specifically, I request that you take the following action(s):

Please respond to this letter within ___ days. I look forward to hearing from you regarding this problem. Please contact the undersigned if you have questions or need additional information.

Sincerely,

_____ (Name and Address)

This page intentionally blank.

PERSONAL PROPERTY LEASE AGREEMENT

This agreement is made by and between _____
_____(the "Lessor") and _____
_____ (the "Lessee").

1. The Lessor hereby leases to the Lessee, and the Lessee hereby leases from the lessor, beginning on _____ and terminating on _____, the property described below (the "Property"):

2. The Lessee shall pay to the Lessor as rent the sum of $_____ per month payable in advance on or before the _____ day of each month, the first such payment being due on _____. Payment of rent shall be made to the Lessor at the following address: _____.

3. The Lessee agrees to use the Property in a careful manner and in compliance with applicable laws and regulations, and at the end of the lease term shall return the Property to the Lessor in the same condition as it was received by the Lessee, normal wear and tear excepted.

4. The Lessor shall not be liable for any liability, loss, or damage caused by the Property or its use that does not result directly and wholly from the negligence of the Lessor.

5. This agreement shall be governed by the laws of _____.

6. If any part of this agreement is adjudged invalid, illegal, or unenforceable, the remaining parts shall not be affected and shall remain in full force and effect.

7. This agreement shall be binding upon the parties, and upon their heirs, executors, personal representatives, administrators, and assigns. No person shall have a right or cause of action arising out of or resulting from this agreement except those who are parties to it and their successors in interest.

8. This instrument, including any attached exhibits and addenda, constitutes the entire agreement of the parties. No representations or promises have been made except those that are set out in this agreement. This agreement may not be modified except in writing signed by all the parties.

IN WITNESS WHEREOF the parties have signed this agreement under seal on _____.

Lessor: Lessee:

_____   _____

_____   _____

This page intentionally blank.

RESIDENTIAL LEASE AGREEMENT

In consideration of the rent reserved and the mutual promises made by the parties to this agreement, _____ (the "Landlord") hereby agrees to rent to _____ (the "Tenant"), and Tenant hereby agrees to rent from Landlord the premises described below (the "Premises") upon the following terms and conditions:

1. **Premises.** The premises referred to in this agreement shall be the property described below:

2. **Term.** The term of this lease shall begin on _____, and expire on _____ (the "Initial Term"). Either Landlord or Tenant may terminate the tenancy at the expiration of the Initial Term by giving written notice to the other at least thirty days prior to the expiration date of the Initial Term. In the event such written notice is not given or if the Tenant holds over beyond the Initial Term, the tenancy shall automatically become a month-to-month tenancy upon the same terms and conditions contained herein and may thereafter be terminated by either Landlord or Tenant by giving the other thirty days' written notice prior to the last day of the then-current period of the tenancy.

3. **Rent.** During the tenancy created by this Agreement:

   3.1 Tenant shall pay, without notice, demand, or deduction to Landlord or as Landlord directs, monthly rental in the amount of $_____ per month during the Initial Term. The first rental payment, which shall be prorated if the Initial Term commences on a day other than the first day of the applicable rental payment period, shall be due at the commencement of the Initial Term and shall constitute payment for the period ending on the first day of the month following the month in which the Initial Term commences. Thereafter all rentals shall be paid in advance on or before the first day of each subsequent calendar month for the duration of the tenancy.

   3.2 In addition to, and as a part of such rent, if any installment of rent is not received within five days of the date it is due, or if Tenant's check shall be returned for insufficient funds, Tenant shall pay as additional rent a late payment fee of $_____, which additional rent shall be due immediately without demand therefor and shall be added to and paid as a part of the installment payment of rent with respect to which it is incurred. Tenant under-stands and agrees that the additional rent shall constitute liquidated damages to reimburse Landlord for expenses and other damages incurred by Landlord as a result of Tenant's late payment of the rental installment.

3.3 Following the Initial Term, the Landlord may from time to time, at his/her option, and upon thirty days' notice to Tenant, increase the monthly rent here-under.

4. **Security Deposit.** Upon execution of this Agreement, the Tenant shall deposit with the Landlord the sum of $_____ ($_____ regular security deposit plus $_____ pet deposit) to secure the faithful performance of the Tenant's promises and duties contained herein (the "Security Deposit"). The Security Deposit shall be held, and upon the termination of the tenancy be applied, in the manner and for the purposes set forth below:

4.1 Upon any termination of the Tenancy created in this agreement, the Landlord may deduct from the Security Deposit amounts sufficient to pay:

4.1.1 Any damages sustained by the Landlord as a result of the Tenant's non-payment of rent or nonfulfillment of the Initial Term or any renewal peri-ods including the Tenant's failure to enter into possession;

4.1.2 Any damages to the Premises for which the Tenant, guests of the Tenant, or pets of the Tenant are responsible;

4.1.3 Any unpaid bills that become a lien against the Premises due to the Tenant's occupancy;

4.1.4 Any costs of rerenting the Premises after a breach of this Agreement by the Tenant;

4.1.5 Any court costs incurred by the Landlord in connection with terminating the tenancy; and,

4.1.6 Any other damages of the Landlord that may then be a permitted use of the Security Deposit under applicable law.

4.2 After having deducted the above amounts, the Landlord shall, if the Tenant's address is known to him or her, refund to the Tenant, within thirty days after the termination of the tenancy and delivery of possession, the balance of the Security Deposit along with an itemized statement of any deductions.

4.3 If the Tenant's address is unknown to the Landlord, the Landlord may deduct the above amounts and shall then hold the balance of the Security Deposit for the Tenant's collection for a six-month period beginning upon the termination of the tenancy and delivery of possession by the Tenant. If the Tenant fails to make demand for the balance of the Security Deposit within the six-month period, the Landlord shall not thereafter be liable to the Tenant for a refund of the Security Deposit or any part thereof.

4.4 The Tenant shall in no circumstance be entitled to receive interest on the Security Deposit.

5. **Assignment.** The Tenant shall not assign this Agreement or sublet the Premises in whole or in part.

6. **Tenant's Duties Upon Termination.** Upon any termination of the tenancy created hereunder, whether by the Landlord or the Tenant, and whether for breach or otherwise, the Tenant shall:

6.1 Pay all utility bills due for services to the Premises for which Tenant is responsible;

6.2 Have all such utility services discontinued, or, at the Landlord's option, transferred into the name of the Landlord or a person designated by the Landlord;

6.3 Vacate the Premises, removing therefrom all Tenant's personal property of whatever nature;

6.4 Properly sweep and clean the Premises, including plumbing fixtures, refrigerators, stoves, and sinks, removing therefrom all rubbish, trash, and refuse, failing which, the Tenant shall become liable to the Landlord, without notice or demand, for a cleaning fee of $_____;

6.5 Make such repairs and perform such other acts as are necessary to return the Premises, and any appliances or fixtures furnished in connection therewith, in the same condition as when this Agreement was executed, ordinary wear and tear excepted;

6.6 Fasten and lock all doors and windows;

6.7 Return to the Landlord the keys to the Premises; and,

6.8 Notify the Landlord of the address to which the balance of the Security Deposit may be returned.

7. **Acceptance of Premises.** The Tenant acknowledges that he/she has inspected the Premises and he/she agrees that the Premises and any common areas used in connection with them are in a safe, fit, and habitable condition and, where applicable, that the electrical, plumbing, sanitary, heating, ventilating, air-conditioning, and other appliances furnished with the Premises are in a good and proper working order. The Tenant also acknowledges that no representation as to the condition or state of repair of the Premises has been made.

8. **Landlord's Obligations.** Unless otherwise agreed upon, the Landlord shall:

   8.1 Comply with the applicable building and housing codes to the extent required by such building and housing codes;

   8.2 Make all repairs to the Premises as may be necessitated by ordinary wear and tear to keep the Premises in a fit and habitable condition. The Landlord shall not, however, be required to make any repairs necessitated by the Tenant's intentional or negligent misuse of the Premises;

   8.3 Keep all common areas, if any, used in conjunction with the Premises in a clean and safe condition; and,

   8.4 Promptly repair all facilities and appliances as may be furnished by the Landlord as part of the Premises, including electrical, plumbing, sanitary, heating (excluding the fireplace), ventilating, and air-conditioning systems, provided that the Landlord actually receives notification from the Tenant in writing of the needed repairs and provided further that the Landlord shall not be required to repair damage to any facility or appliance that is caused by the Tenant's deliberate or negligent misuse or improper operation of them.

9. **Tenant's Obligations.** Unless otherwise agreed upon, the Tenant shall:

   9.1 Use the Premises for residential purposes for not more than _____ persons only and in a manner so as not to disturb his/her neighbors;

   9.2 Not use the Premises for any unlawful or immoral purposes or occupy them in such a way as to constitute a nuisance;

   9.3 Keep the Premises, including but not limited to, all plumbing fixtures, facilities and appliances, and any common areas and yards used by him/her in connection with the Premises in a clean, safe, sanitary, and presentable condition;

   9.4 Comply with any and all obligations imposed upon tenants by applicable building and housing codes;

9.5 Use in a proper, reasonable, and careful manner all electrical, plumbing, sanitary, heating, ventilating, air-conditioning, and other facilities and appliances (including, should the tenant chose to use it, the fireplace) furnished as a part of the Premises, and Tenant shall be liable to Landlord for any damages caused by his/her failure to comply with this requirement;

9.6 Dispose of all ashes, rubbish, garbage, and other waste in a clean and safe manner and comply with all applicable ordinances concerning garbage collection, waste, and other refuse;

9.7 Not deliberately or negligently destroy, deface, damage, or remove any part of the Premises (including all facilities, appliances, and fixtures) or permit any person, known or unknown to the Tenant, to do so;

9.8 Be responsible for and liable to the Landlord for all damage, to defacement of, or removal of property from the Premises whatever the cause, except such damage, defacement, or removal caused by ordinary wear and tear, acts of the Landlord, his/her agent, or of third parties not invitees of the Tenant, and natural forces;

9.9 Permit the Landlord (and the Landlord hereby reserves the right) to enter the Premises during reasonable hours for the purpose of:

9.9.1 Inspecting the Premises and the Tenant's compliance with the terms of this Agreement;

9.9.2 Making such repairs, alterations, improvements, or additions thereto as the Landlord may deem appropriate; and,

9.9.3 Showing the Premises to prospective purchasers or tenants (the Landlord shall have the right to display "For Sale" or "For Rent" signs in a reasonable manner upon the Premises);

9.10 Pay the costs of all utility services to the Premises that are billed directly to the Tenant and not included as a part of the rentals, including, but not limited to, water, electric, telephone, cable, and gas or oil services;

9.11 Conduct him- or herself and require all other persons on the Premises with Tenant's consent to conduct themselves in a reasonable manner and so as not to disturb his/her neighbors' peaceful enjoyment of the Premises; and,

9.12 Not abandon or vacate the Premises during the Initial Term or any renewals or extensions thereof. The Tenant shall be deemed to have abandoned or vacated the Premises if Tenant removes substantially all his/her possessions from the Premises. In addition, if Tenant is absent from the Premises for ten consecutive days while a rental payment is delinquent, he/she shall be deemed to have abandoned or vacated the Premises effective the first day of such ten-day period of absence.

10. **Tenant's Default.** In the event the Tenant shall (a) fail to pay the rentals herein reserved as and when the same shall become due hereunder; or, (b) fail to perform any other promise, duty, or obligation herein agreed to by him/her or imposed upon him/her by law, and such failure shall continue for a period of five days from the date the Landlord provides Tenant with written notice of such failure; then in either of such events and as often as either of them may occur, the Landlord, in addition to all other rights and remedies provided by law, may, at its option and with or without notice to Tenant, either (a) terminate this Agreement or (b) terminate the Tenant's right to possession of the Premises without terminating this Agreement.

10.1 Regardless of whether Landlord terminates this Agreement or only terminates the Tenant's right of possession without terminating this Agreement, Landlord shall be immediately entitled to possession of the premises and the Tenant shall peacefully surrender possession of the Premises to Landlord immediately upon Landlord's demand. In the event Tenant shall fail or refuse to surrender possession of the Premises, Landlord shall, in compliance with applicable law, reenter and retake possession of the Premises.

10.2 In the event Landlord terminates this Agreement, all further rights and duties hereunder shall terminate and Landlord shall be entitled to collect from Tenant all accrued but unpaid rents and any damages resulting from the Tenant's breach.

10.3 In the event Landlord terminates the Tenant's right of possession without terminating this Agreement, Tenant shall remain liable for the full performance of all the covenants hereof, and Landlord shall use reasonable efforts to relet the Premises on Tenant's behalf. Any such rentals reserved from such reletting shall be applied first to the costs of reletting the Premises and then to the rentals due hereunder. In the event the rentals from such reletting are insufficient to pay the rentals due hereunder in full, Tenant shall be liable to the Landlord for any deficiency.

10.4 In the event Landlord institutes a legal action against the Tenant to enforce this Agreement or to recover any sums due hereunder, Tenant agrees to pay

Landlord reasonable attorney's fees in addition to all other damages. The Landlord's damages shall in no way be limited by the amount of the Security Deposit described in paragraph 4.

11. **Landlord's Default, Limitations of Remedies, and Damages.** No defaults by the Landlord in the performance of any of the promises or obligations herein agreed to by him/her or imposed upon him/her by law shall constitute a material breach of this agreement, and the Tenant shall have no right to terminate this Agreement for any such default or suspend his/her performance hereunder, until the Tenant notifies the Landlord in writing of the alleged default and affords the Landlord a reasonable time within which to cure the default.

   11.1 In no event and regardless of their duration, shall any defective condition or conditions of or failure or failures to repair, maintain, or provide any common area, fixture, or facility used in connection with the Premises, including, but not limited to, parking areas or garages, constitute a material breach of this Agreement and the Tenant shall have no right to terminate this Agreement or to suspend his/her performance hereunder.

   11.2 In any legal action instituted by the Tenant against the Landlord, whether for partial or material breach or breaches of this Agreement or any obligation imposed by law upon the Landlord, the Tenant's damages shall be limited to the difference, if any, between the rent reserved in this Agreement and the reasonable rental value of the Premises, taking into account the Landlord's breach or breaches, and in no event shall the Tenant collect any consequential or secondary damages resulting from the breach or breaches, including but not limited to the following items: injury or destruction of furniture or other personal property of any kind located in or about the Premises, moving expenses, storage expenses, alternative interim housing expenses, and expenses of locating and procuring alternative housing.

12. **Alterations.** The Tenant shall not paint or decorate the Premises or make any alterations, additions, or improvements in or to the Premises without the Landlord's prior written consent and then only in a workmanlike manner using materials and contractors approved by the Landlord. All such work shall be done at the Tenant's expense and at such times and in such manner as the Landlord may approve. All alterations, additions, and improvements upon the Premises, made by either the Landlord or Tenant, shall become the property of the Landlord and shall remain upon and become a part of the Premises at the end of the tenancy hereby created.

13. **Waiver.** No waiver of any breach of any obligation or promise contained herein shall be regarded as a waiver of any future breach of the same or any other obligation or promise.

14. **Form and Interpretation.** In construing this Agreement, the following rules shall be applied.

    14.1 Paragraph headings are used only for convenience of reference and shall not be considered as a substantive part of this Agreement.

    14.2 Words in the singular shall include the plural, and the masculine shall include the feminine and neuter genders, as appropriate.

    14.3 The invalidity of one or more provisions of this Agreement shall not affect the validity of any other provisions hereof and this Agreement shall be construed and enforced as if such invalid provision(s) were not included.

    14.4 If two or more persons are tenants hereunder, then the term "Tenant" shall refer to all such persons individually and collectively and their duties, obligations, and liabilities hereunder shall be joint and several.

15. **Notices.** Any notices required or authorized to be given hereunder or pursuant to applicable law shall be mailed or hand-delivered to the following addresses:

    15.1 To Tenant at the address of the Premises.

    15.2 To Landlord at the address to which rental payments are sent.

16. **Eminent Domain and Casualties.** The Landlord shall have the option to terminate this Agreement if the Premises, or any part thereof, are condemned or sold in lieu of condemnation or damaged by fire or other casualty.

17. **Tenant's Insurance, Release, and Indemnity Provisions.** The Tenant shall insure any of his/her personal property located or stored upon the Premises against the risks of damage, destruction, or loss resulting from theft, fire, storm, and all other hazards and casualties. Such insurance shall be in an amount equal to the replacement value of the property so insured and shall be placed in such companies as are selected by the Tenant. Regardless of whether the Tenant secures such insurance, the Landlord and his/her agents shall not be liable for any damage to, destruction of, or loss of any of the Tenant's personal property located or stored upon the Premises regardless of the cause or causes of such damage, destruction, or loss. The Tenant agrees to release and indemnify the Landlord and his/her agents from and against liability for injury to the person of the Tenant or

to any members of his/her household resulting from any cause whatsoever except only such personal injury caused by the negligent or intentional acts of the Landlord.

18. **Counterparts.** This Agreement is executed under seal this ____ day of _____, 20___, in two counterparts with an executed counterpart being retained by each party to the Agreement.

Tenant: Landlord:

_____   _____

This page intentionally blank.

COMMERCIAL LEASE AGREEMENT

In Consideration of the rent reserved and the mutual promises made by the parties to this agreement, _____ (the "Landlord") hereby agrees to rent to _____ (the "Tenant"), and Tenant hereby agrees to rent from Landlord the premises described below (the "Premises") upon the following terms and conditions:

1. **Premises and Use.** The Premises referred to in this agreement shall be the property containing _____ square feet of space located at:

   The Premises shall be used by the Tenant only for the purpose of:

2. **Term.** The term of this lease shall begin on _____ and expire on _____ (the "Initial Term"). Either Landlord or Tenant may terminate the tenancy at the expiration of the Initial Term by giving written notice to the other at least thirty days prior to the expiration date of the Initial Term. In the event such written notice is not given or if the Tenant holds over beyond the Initial Term, the tenancy shall automatically become a month-to-month tenancy upon the same terms and conditions contained herein and may thereafter be terminated by either Landlord or Tenant by giving the other thirty days' written notice prior to the last day of the then-current period of the tenancy.

3. **Rent.** During the tenancy created by this Agreement:

   3.1 Tenant shall pay, without notice, demand, or deduction to Landlord or as Landlord directs, monthly rental in the amount of $_____ per month during the Initial Term. The first rental payment, which shall be prorated if the Initial Term commences on a day other than the first day of the applicable rental payment period, shall be due at the commencement of the Initial Term and shall constitute payment for the period ending on the first day of the month following the month in which the Initial Term commences.

Thereafter all rentals shall be paid in advance on or before the first day of each subsequent calendar month for the duration of the tenancy.

3.2 In addition to, and as a part of such rent, if any installment of rent is not received within five days of the date it is due, or if Tenant's check shall be returned for insufficient funds, Tenant shall pay as additional rent a late payment fee of $_____, which additional rent shall be due immediately without demand therefor and shall be added to and paid as a part of the installment payment of rent with respect to which it is incurred. Tenant understands and agrees that the additional rent shall constitute liquidated damages to reimburse Landlord for expenses and other damages incurred by Landlord as a result of Tenant's late payment of the rental installment.

3.3 Following the Initial Term, the Landlord may from time to time, at his/her/its option, and upon thirty days' notice to Tenant, increase the monthly rent hereunder.

4. **Security Deposit.** Upon execution of this Agreement, the Tenant shall deposit with the Landlord the sum of $_____ to secure the faithful performance of the Tenant's promises and duties contained herein (the "Security Deposit"). The Security Deposit shall be held, and upon the termination of the tenancy be applied, in the manner and for the purposes set forth below.

4.1 Upon any termination of the Tenancy created in this agreement, the Landlord may deduct from the Security Deposit amounts sufficient to pay:

4.1.1 Any damages sustained by the Landlord as a result of the Tenant's non-payment of rent or nonfulfillment of the Initial Term or any renewal periods including the Tenant's failure to enter into possession;

4.1.2 Any damages to the Premises for which the Tenant or its employees, invitees or licensees are responsible;

4.1.3 Any unpaid bills that become a lien against the Premises due to the Tenant's occupancy;

4.1.4 Any costs of rerenting the Premises after a breach of this Agreement by the Tenant;

4.1.5 Any court costs incurred by the Landlord in connection with terminating the tenancy; and,

4.1.6 Any other damages of the Landlord that may then be a permitted use of the Security Deposit under applicable law.

4.2 After having deducted the above amounts, the Landlord shall, if the Tenant's address is known to him or her, refund to the Tenant, within thirty days after the termination of the tenancy and delivery of possession, the balance of the Security Deposit along with an itemized statement of any deductions.

4.3 If the Tenant's address is unknown to the Landlord, the Landlord may deduct the above amounts and shall then hold the balance of the Security Deposit for the Tenant's collection for a six-month period beginning upon the termination of the tenancy and delivery of possession by the Tenant. If the Tenant fails to make demand for the balance of the Security Deposit within the six-month period, the Landlord shall not thereafter be liable to the Tenant for a refund of the Security Deposit or any part thereof.

4.4 The Tenant shall in no circumstance be entitled to receive interest on the Security Deposit.

5. **Assignment.** The Tenant shall not assign this Agreement or sublet the Premises in whole or in part. If the Tenant is a corporation, limited partnership, or limited liability company, the sale or encumbrance of a majority of its outstanding voting stock, memberships, or other ownership interests shall be deemed to be an assignment of this lease.

6. **Tenant's Duties Upon Termination.** Upon any termination of the tenancy created hereunder, whether by the Landlord or the Tenant, and whether for breach or otherwise, the Tenant shall:

6.1 Pay all utility bills due for services to the Premises for which Tenant is responsible;

6.2 Have all such utility services discontinued, or, at the Landlord's option, transferred into the name of the Landlord or a person designated by the Landlord;

6.3 Vacate the Premises removing therefrom all Tenant's personal property of whatever nature; provided, however, that Tenant hereby covenants and agrees that all additions and other improvements installed in the demised premises by Tenant, including, without limitation, all electric wiring, electric fixtures, air-conditioning systems, and carpeting, shall immediately become the property of Landlord and shall not be removed by Tenant unless requested to do so by

Landlord, in which event Tenant agrees to do so and to repair promptly any damage caused by any such removal.

6.4 Properly sweep and clean the Premises, including plumbing and other fixtures, removing therefrom all rubbish, trash, and refuse, failing which the Tenant shall become liable to the Landlord, without notice or demand, for a cleaning fee of $_____ ;

6.5 Make such repairs and perform such other acts as are necessary to return the Premises, and any appliances or fixtures furnished in connection therewith, in the same condition as when this Agreement was executed, ordinary wear and tear excepted;

6.6 Fasten and lock all doors and windows;

6.7 Return to the Landlord the keys to the Premises; and,

6.8 Notify the Landlord of the address to which the balance of the Security Deposit may be returned.

7. **Acceptance of Premises.** The Tenant acknowledges that he/she has inspected the Premises and he/she agrees that the Premises and any common areas used in connection with them are in a safe, fit, and habitable condition and, where applicable, that the electrical, plumbing, sanitary, heating, ventilating, air-conditioning, and other appliances furnished with the Premises are in a good and proper working order. The Tenant also acknowledges that no representation as to the condition or state of repair of the Premises has been made.

8. **Landlord's Obligations.** Unless otherwise agreed upon, the Landlord shall:

8.1 Comply with the applicable building codes to the extent required by such codes; and,

8.2 Keep all common areas, if any, used in conjunction with the Premises in a clean and safe condition.

9. **Tenant's Obligations.** Unless otherwise agreed upon by Landlord and Tenant, the Tenant shall:

9.1 Use the Premises for the purpose stated in paragraph 1 above and for no other purpose;

9.2 Not use the Premises for any unlawful or immoral purposes or occupy them in such a way as to constitute a nuisance;

9.3 Keep the Premises, including, but not limited to, all plumbing fixtures, facilities and appliances, and any common areas and yards used by him/her/it in connection with the Premises in a clean, safe, sanitary, and presentable condition;

9.4 Comply with any and all obligations imposed upon tenants by applicable building codes and local, state, and federal laws, rules, ordinances, and regulations;

9.5 Use in a proper, reasonable, and careful manner all electrical, plumbing, sanitary, heating, ventilating, air-conditioning, and other facilities and appliances, located at the Premises, and Tenant shall be liable to Landlord for any damages caused by his/her/its failure to comply with this requirement;

9.6 Dispose of all refuse, rubbish, garbage, and other waste in a clean and safe manner and comply with all applicable ordinances concerning garbage collection, waste, and other refuse;

9.7 Not deliberately or negligently destroy, deface, damage, or remove any part of the Premises (including all facilities, appliances, and fixtures) or permit any person, known or unknown to the Tenant, to do so;

9.8 Be responsible for and liable to the Landlord for all damage, to defacement of, or removal of property from the Premises whatever the cause, except such damage, defacement, or removal caused by ordinary wear and tear and natural forces;

9.9 Permit the Landlord (and the Landlord hereby reserves the right) to enter the Premises during reasonable hours for the purpose of:

9.9.1 Inspecting the Premises and the Tenant's compliance with the terms of this Agreement;

9.9.2 Making such repairs, alterations, improvements, or additions thereto as the Landlord may deem appropriate; and,

9.9.3 Showing the Premises to prospective purchasers or tenants (the Landlord shall have the right to display "For Sale" or "For Rent" signs in a reasonable manner upon the Premises);

9.10 Pay the costs of all utility services to the Premises, including, but not limited to, water, electric, telephone, cable, and gas or oil services;

9.11 Conduct him- or herself and require all other persons on the Premises with Tenant's consent to conduct themselves in a reasonable manner and so as not to create a nuisance; and,

9.12 Not abandon or vacate the Premises during the Initial Term or any renewals or extensions thereof. The Tenant shall be deemed to have abandoned or vacated the Premises if Tenant removes substantially all his/her/its possessions from the Premises.

9.13 Not permit any mechanic's, materialman's, or similar lien to stand against any portion of the premises for any labor or material furnished in connection with any work performed or caused to be performed by the Tenant.

9.14 Within ten days of a request by the Landlord, certify by a duly executed and acknowledged written instrument to any person designated by the Landlord, as to the validity and force and effect of this lease, as to the existence of any default on the part of any party thereunder, as to the existence of any offsets, counterclaims, or defenses on the part of Tenant, and as to any other matters as may be reasonably requested by the Landlord.

9.15 Make all repairs to the Premises except as may be necessitated by ordinary wear and tear to keep the Premises in a fit and habitable condition; provided, however, that Landlord shall be responsible for maintenance and repair of the roof and exterior walls. The Landlord shall not, however, be required to make any repairs necessitated by the Tenant's intentional or negligent misuse of the Premises.

9.16 Promptly repair all facilities and appliances that are a part of the Premises, including electrical, plumbing, sanitary, heating, ventilating, and air-conditioning systems.

10. **Tenant's Default.** In the event the Tenant shall (a) fail to pay the rentals herein reserved as and when the same shall become due hereunder; or, (b) fail to perform any other promise, duty, or obligation herein agreed to by him/her/it or imposed upon him/her/it by law, and such failure shall continue for a period of five days from the date the Landlord provides Tenant with written notice of such failure; then in either of such events and as often as either of them may occur, the Landlord, in addition to all other rights and remedies provided by law, may, at its option and with or without notice to Tenant, either (a) terminate this Agreement or (b) terminate the Tenant's right to possession of the Premises without terminating this Agreement.

10.1 Regardless of whether Landlord terminates this Agreement or only terminates the Tenant's right of possession without terminating this Agreement, Landlord shall be immediately entitled to possession of the premises and the Tenant shall peacefully surrender possession of the Premises to Landlord immediately upon Landlord's demand. In the event Tenant shall fail or refuse to surrender possession of the Premises, Landlord shall, in compliance with applicable law, reenter and retake possession of the Premises.

10.2 In the event Landlord terminates this Agreement, all further rights and duties hereunder shall terminate and Landlord shall be entitled to collect from Tenant all accrued but unpaid rents and any damages resulting from the Tenant's breach.

10.3 In the event Landlord terminates the Tenant's right of possession without terminating this Agreement, Tenant shall remain liable for the full performance of all the covenants hereof, and Landlord shall use reasonable efforts to relet the Premises on Tenant's behalf. Any such rentals reserved from such reletting shall be applied first to the costs of reletting the Premises and then to the rentals due hereunder. In the event the rentals from such reletting are insufficient to pay the rentals due hereunder in full, Tenant shall be liable to the Landlord for any deficiency.

10.4 In the event Landlord institutes a legal action against the Tenant to enforce this Agreement or to recover any sums due hereunder, Tenant agrees to pay Landlord reasonable attorney's fees in addition to all other damages. The Landlord's damages shall in no way be limited by the amount of the Security Deposit described in paragraph 4.

11. **Landlord's Default, Limitations of Remedies, and Damages.** No defaults by the Landlord in the performance of any of the promises or obligations herein agreed to by him/her/it or imposed upon him/her/it by law shall constitute a material breach of this agreement, and the Tenant shall have no right to terminate this Agreement for any such default or suspend his/her performance hereunder, until the Tenant notifies the Landlord in writing of the alleged default and affords the Landlord a reasonable time within which to cure the default.

11.1 In no event and regardless of their duration, shall any defective condition or conditions of or failure or failures to repair, maintain, or provide any common area, fixture, or facility used in connection with the Premises, including, but not limited to, parking areas or garages, constitute a material breach of this

Agreement, and the Tenant shall have no right to terminate this Agreement or to suspend his/her performance hereunder.

11.2 In any legal action instituted by the Tenant against the Landlord, whether for partial or material breach or breaches of this Agreement or any obligation imposed by law upon the Landlord, the Tenant's damages shall be limited to the difference, if any, between the rent reserved in this Agreement and the reasonable rental value of the Premises, taking into account the Landlord's breach or breaches, and in no event shall the Tenant collect any consequential or secondary damages resulting from the breach or breaches, including, but not limited to, the following items: injury or destruction of furniture or other personal property of any kind located in or about the Premises, moving expenses, storage expenses, alternative interim housing expenses, and expenses of locating and procuring alternative housing.

12. **Alterations.** The Tenant shall not paint or decorate the Premises or make any alterations, additions, or improvements in or to the Premises without the Landlord's prior written consent and then only in a workmanlike manner using materials and contractors approved by the Landlord. All such work shall be done at the Tenant's expense and at such times and in such manner as the Landlord may approve. All alterations, additions, and improvements upon the Premises, made by either the Landlord or Tenant, shall become the property of the Landlord and shall remain upon and become a part of the Premises at the end of the tenancy hereby created.

13. **Waiver.** No waiver of any breach of any obligation or promise contained herein shall be regarded as a waiver of any future breach of the same or any other obligation or promise.

14. **Form and Interpretation.** In construing this Agreement, the following rules shall be applied:

14.1 Paragraph headings are used only for convenience of reference and shall not be considered as a substantive part of this Agreement.

14.2 Words in the singular shall include the plural and the masculine shall include the feminine and neuter genders, as appropriate.

14.3 The invalidity of one or more provisions of this Agreement shall not affect the validity of any other provisions hereof and this Agreement shall be construed and enforced as if such invalid provision(s) were not included.

14.4 If two or more persons are tenants hereunder, then the term "Tenant" shall refer to all such persons individually and collectively and their duties, obligations, and liabilities hereunder shall be joint and several.

15. **Notices.** Any notices required or authorized to be given hereunder or pursuant to applicable law shall be mailed or hand-delivered to the following addresses:

    15.1 To Tenant at the address of the Premises.

    15.2 To Landlord at the address to which rental payments are sent.

16. **Eminent Domain and Casualties.** The Landlord shall have the option to terminate this Agreement if the Premises, or any part thereof, are condemned or sold in lieu of condemnation or damaged by fire or other casualty.

17. **Tenant's Insurance, Release, and Indemnity Provisions.** The Tenant shall insure any of his/her/its personal property located or stored upon the premises against the risks of damage, destruction, or loss resulting from theft, fire, storm, and all other hazards and casualties. Such insurance shall be in an amount equal to the replacement value of the property so insured and shall be placed in such companies as are selected by the Tenant. Regardless of whether the Tenant secures such insurance, the Landlord and his/her/its agents shall not be liable for any damage to, destruction of, or loss of any of the Tenant's personal property located or stored upon the Premises regardless of the cause or causes of such damage, destruction, or loss. The Tenant agrees to release and indemnify the Landlord and his/her/its agents from and against liability for injury to the person of the Tenant or to any members of his/her household resulting from any cause whatsoever except only such personal injury caused by the negligent or intentional acts of the Landlord.

18. **Counterparts.** This Agreement is executed under seal this ____ day of _____, 20___, in two counterparts with an executed counterpart being retained by each party to the Agreement.

Tenant: Landlord:

_____   _____

This page intentionally blank.

LEASE ASSIGNMENT

This Lease Assignment is entered into by and among _____ (the "Assignor"), _____ (the "Assignee"), and _____ (the "Landlord"). For valuable consideration, it is agreed by the parties as follows:

1. The Landlord and the Assignor have entered into a lease agreement (the "Lease") dated _____, concerning the premises described as:

2. The Assignor hereby assigns and transfers to the Assignee all of Assignor's rights and delegates all of Assignor's duties under the Lease effective _____ (the "Effective Date").

3. The Assignee hereby accepts such assignment of rights and delegation of duties and agrees to pay all rents promptly when due and perform all of Assignor's obligations under the Lease accruing on and after the Effective Date. The Assignee further agrees to indemnify and hold the Assignor harmless from any breach of Assignee's duties hereunder.

4. ❑ The Assignor agrees to transfer possession of the leased premises to the Assignee on the Effective Date. All rents and obligations of the Assignor under the Lease accruing before the Effective Date shall have been paid or discharged.

   ❑ The Landlord hereby assents to the assignment of the Lease hereunder and as of the Effective Date hereby releases and discharges the Assignor from all duties and obligations under the Lease accruing after the Effective Date.

   ❑ The Landlord hereby assents to this lease assignment provided that the Landlord's assent shall not discharge the Assignor of any obligations under the Lease in the event of breach by the Assignee. The Landlord will give notice to the Assignor of any breach by the Assignee. If the Assignor pays all accrued rents and cures any other default of the Assignee, the Assignor may enforce the terms of the Lease and this Assignment against the Assignee, in the name of the Landlord, if necessary.

5. There shall be no further assignment of the Lease without the written consent of the Landlord.

6. This agreement shall be binding upon and inure to the benefit of the parties, their successors, assigns, and personal representatives.

This assignment was executed under seal on _____.

Assignor: Assignee:

_____   _____

_____   _____

Landlord:

_____

_____

ESTOPPEL LETTER

Date _____

To:

Re: Estoppel Certificate

Dear Sir or Madam:

The undersigned is Tenant under a lease dated _____ (the "Lease") related to property (the "Premises") located at:

The Landlord under the Lease is _____.

The Tenant under the Lease is _____.

The undersigned Tenant hereby certifies as follows:

1. The Lease constitutes the complete agreement regarding the Premises between the Landlord and the Tenant. There are no other agreements, provisions, options, or rights existing between Landlord and Tenant with respect to the Premises, except as contained in the Lease.

2. The Landlord is in possession of $_____ as security for the performance of the Tenant's obligations under the lease.

3. The term of the Lease commenced on (date) _____ and will expire on (date) _____. The Lease may be extended beyond such term under the following   conditions:

    _____

4. The monthly rent payable under the Lease is _____. The following additional rent is payable (if any): _____
_____. The
Tenant has paid all rent due through (date) _____.

5. The Lease is, at the date of this letter, in full force and effect and, to the best knowledge of the Tenant, no default exists on the part of the Landlord or the Tenant. The Tenant has no claims, offsets, credits, deductions, or other defenses as to the payment of rent or the performance of Tenant's duties under the Lease.

This certification is made by the Tenant with the understanding that Landlord and the addressee of this letter has the right to rely on such certification in connection with the following transaction(s):

Name of Tenant: _____

By: _____

Printed or typed name and title: _____

AMENDMENT TO REAL PROPERTY LEASE AGREEMENT

For valuable consideration, the receipt and sufficiency of which is hereby acknowledged by each of the parties, this agreement amends a lease agreement (the "Lease") between _____ (the "Landlord") and _____ (the "Tenant") dated_____, relating to property located at _____ _____.

This agreement is hereby incorporated into the Lease.

Except as changed by this amendment, the Lease shall continue in effect according to its terms. The amendments herein shall be effective on the date this document is executed by both parties.

Executed on _____.

Landlord: Tenant:

_____   _____

_____   _____

This page intentionally blank.

LANDLORD'S CONSENT TO SUBLEASE

FOR VALUABLE CONSIDERATION, the undersigned (the "Landlord") hereby consents to the sublease of all or part of the premises located at _____ _____, which is the subject of a lease agreement between Landlord and _____ (the "Tenant"), pursuant to an Agreement to Sublease dated _____, between the Tenant and _____ as Subtenant dated _____.

This consent was signed by the Landlord on _____.

Landlord:

_____

This page intentionally blank.

RENTER'S DEMAND FOR ACTION BY LANDLORD

Date: _____

To:

Dear Sir or Madam:

This letter will serve to notify you that:

According to the terms of the lease dated _____ between you as Landlord and the undersigned as Tenant, you are required to take the following action:

This action is required pursuant to the sections or paragraphs listed below:

I have previously contacted you about this problem in the ways and on the dates listed below:

Please correct this problem as soon as possible. If no action is taken by you within _____ days, I will consider further actions to enforce the terms of the lease or otherwise enforce the rights of the undersigned pursuant to applicable law.

Sincerely,

_____ (Tenant)

_____ (Address)

_____

_____

This page intentionally blank.

AGREEMENT TO CANCEL LEASE

On _____ (date of Lease), _____ (the "Landlord")
and _____ (the "Tenant") entered into a lease agreement
related to real property described below (the "Lease Agreement"):

Landlord and Tenant hereby mutually agree that the Lease Agreement shall terminate
on _____ (revised termination date). Except for the revised date of
termination, all other provisions of the Lease Agreement, including default remedies,
will continue in effect according to its terms.

The date of this agreement is _____.

Landlord: Tenant:

_____   _____

This page intentionally blank.

ASSIGNMENT OF COPYRIGHT

This Assignment is made this _____ day of _____, _____, between _____ as Owner of the copyright on the Work known as _____
_____
_____,
and _____ as Purchaser.

WHEREAS the Owner is sole owner of all rights in the Work and whereas the Purchaser is desirous of purchasing all such rights,

IT IS AGREED between the parties hereto that in consideration of the sum of $_____, the receipt of which is hereby acknowledged, the Owner hereby assigns to the Purchaser all his/her interest in the Work and the copyright thereon, which interest shall be held for the full term of said copyright.

IN WITNESS WHEREOF, the Owner has executed this Agreement on the date above written.

_____

STATE OF   )
COUNTY OF   )

I certify that _____, who ❏ is personally known to me to be the person whose name is subscribed to the foregoing instrument ❏ produced _____ as identification, personally appeared before me on _____, and ❏ acknowledged the execution of the foregoing instrument ❏ acknowledged that (s)he is (Assistant) Secretary of _____ and that by authority duly given and as the act of the corporation, the foregoing instrument was signed in its name by its (Vice) President, sealed with its corporate seal, and attested by him/her as its (Assistant) Secretary.

_____
Notary Public, State of

Notary's commission expires:

This page intentionally blank.

COPYRIGHT LICENSE

This License is made this _____ day of _____, between
_____ as Owner of the copyright
on the Work known as _____
and _____ as Licensee.

WHEREAS the Owner is sole owner of all rights in the Work and whereas the Licensee is desirous of purchasing rights in said Work;

IT IS AGREED between the parties hereto that in consideration of the sum of $_____, the receipt of which is hereby acknowledged, the Owner hereby licenses the Licensee to use the copyrighted Work as follows:

It is understood between the parties that this License covers only those uses listed above for the time period stated. All other rights in and to the copyrighted work shall remain the property of the Owner.

This agreement shall be governed by the laws of _____.

If any part of this agreement is adjudged invalid, illegal, or unenforceable, the remaining parts shall not be affected and shall remain in full force and effect.

This agreement shall be binding upon the parties, and upon their heirs, executors, personal representatives, administrators, and assigns. No person shall have a right or cause of action arising out of or resulting from this agreement except those who are parties to it and their successors in interest.

This instrument, including any attached exhibits and addenda, constitutes the entire agreement of the parties. No representations or promises have been made except those that are set out in this agreement. This agreement may not be modified except in writing signed by all the parties.

IN WITNESS WHEREOF the parties have signed this agreement under seal on _____.

Owner: Licensee:

_____   _____

_____   _____

This page intentionally blank.

RESPONSE TO SUBMISSION OF UNSOLICITED IDEAS

From:

To:

Dear _____,

    Thank you for your interest in our company in submitting your material for our review. We receive many ideas, proposals, and other materials, and also have many of our own projects under consideration and development. Therefore, it is possible that what is contained in your submission is already under planning or development, or has previously been considered.

❏   It is our company policy not to accept unsolicited ideas, proposals, or materials; therefore, we are returning your material unopened.

❏   It is our company policy not to accept unsolicited ideas, proposals, or materials; therefore, we are returning your material. Although we prefer to return such materials unopened, it was impossible to know that your package was such a submission until it was opened.

❏   If you would like us to consider your material, you will need to submit it along with an executed and witnessed copy of this form, agreeing to the following terms and conditions:

1. We do not accept any responsibility for loss of the materials you submit, or for keeping your submission confidential, although we will use our best efforts to keep it confidential.

2. Your submission will be returned to you only if you prepay return postage or freight.

3. We agree that this document does not give us any rights in your submission, and we will not exploit your idea, proposal, or material in any way without first entering into an agreement for compensation.

4. We will only pay compensation if all the following applies: a) we accept your idea, proposal, or material; b) we have received the idea, proposal, or material only from you (i.e., we will have no obligation to you if your idea, proposal, or material is currently under consideration, planning, or development by us); and c) we enter into a written agreement with you as to the

terms and conditions for use of your idea, proposal, or material and the compensation to be paid to you.

_____

I understand and agree to the foregoing terms and conditions.

Dated: _____

_____   _____
Witness   Submitter

PERMISSION TO USE QUOTE, PERSONAL STATEMENT, OR OTHER MATERIAL

The undersigned hereby authorizes _____
_____, its successors, and assigns, to use, publish, print, and otherwise communicate, in whole or in part, the following statement, endorsement, quotation, photograph, or other material attached described as:

❏ see copy attached hereto.

This authorization   ❏ is ❏ is not   exclusive.

This authorization   ❏ is unlimited   ❏ is limited as follows:

The undersigned acknowledges that this authorization is irrevocable, and that no other or further payment or consideration is due.

Signed on _____.

_____   _____
Witness   Signature

Name: _____   Name: _____
Address: _____   Address: _____
_____   _____

This page intentionally blank.

MEDIATION AGREEMENT

The undersigned parties are engaged in a dispute regarding _____
_____.
We hereby agree to submit such dispute to mediation by _____
_____ and that all matters resolved
in mediation shall be reduced to a binding written agreement signed by the parties.
The costs of mediation shall be borne equally by the parties.

Dated: _____

_____   _____

_____   _____

This page intentionally blank.

ARBITRATION AGREEMENT

This Arbitration Agreement is made this _____ day of _____, _____, by and between _____ and _____, who agree as follows:

1. The parties agree that any controversy, claim, or dispute arising out of or related to:

shall be submitted to arbitration. Such arbitration shall take place at _____

or at such other place as may be agreed upon by the parties.

2. The parties shall attempt to agree on one arbitrator. If they are unable to so agree, then each party shall appoint one arbitrator and those appointed shall appoint a third arbitrator.

3. The expenses of arbitration shall be divided equally by the parties.

4. The arbitrators shall conclusively decide all issues of law and fact related to the arbitrated dispute. Judgment upon an award rendered by the arbitrator may be entered in any court having jurisdiction.

5. The prevailing party ❏ shall ❏ shall not be entitled to reasonable attorney's fees.

_____   _____

_____   _____

This page intentionally blank.

WAIVER AND ASSUMPTION OF RISK

I, _____,
hereby voluntarily sign this Waiver and Assumption of Risk in favor of
_____ (the "Company"),
fully waiving and releasing the Company from any and all claims for personal injury,
property damage, or death that may result from my use of the Company's facilities or
property, or from my participation in the following activities or instruction ("activities"):

I sign this Waiver and Assumption of Risk in consideration of the opportunity to
use the Company's facilities or property, receive instruction from the Company and its
employees, or to participate in Company-sponsored activities as described above.

I acknowledge and understand that there are dangers and risks associated with
the activities described above, which have been fully explained to me. I fully assume
the dangers and risks, and agree to use my best judgment in engaging in those activities and to follow the safety instructions provided.

I am a competent adult, aged _____, and I freely and voluntarily assume
the risks associated with the activities described above.

Dated: _____

Witness: _____

Name: _____
Address: _____
_____
Telephone: _____

In case of emergency, please contact:

Name: _____
Address: _____
_____
Telephone: _____
Relationship: _____

This page intentionally blank.

GENERAL RELEASE

In exchange for the sum of $10.00 and other valuable consideration, the receipt and sufficiency of which is hereby acknowledged, the undersigned corporation hereby forever releases, discharges, and acquits _____, and [its/his/her] successors, assigns, heirs, and personal representatives, from any and all claims, actions, suits, agreements, or liabilities in favor of or owed to the undersigned, existing at any time up to the date of this release.

IN WITNESS WHEREOF, the undersigned has executed this release under seal on _____.

This page intentionally blank.

SPECIFIC RELEASE

In exchange for the sum of $10.00 and other valuable consideration, the receipt and sufficiency of which is hereby acknowledged, the undersigned hereby forever releases, discharges, and acquits _____,
and [its/his/her] successors, assigns, heirs, and personal representatives, from any and all claims, actions, suits, agreements, or liabilities arising out of or related to:

IN WITNESS WHEREOF, the undersigned has executed this release under seal on
_____.

This page intentionally blank.

MUTUAL RELEASE

In exchange for the sum of $10.00 and other valuable consideration, the receipt and sufficiency of which is hereby acknowledged, the undersigned hereby forever release, discharge, and acquit each other, and their successors, assigns, heirs, and personal representatives, from any and all claims, actions, suits, agreements, or liabilities arising out of or related to:

IN WITNESS WHEREOF, the undersigned have executed this release under seal on _____.

_____   _____

_____   _____

This page intentionally blank.

COVENANT NOT TO SUE

This agreement is made by and between _____ (the "Covenantor"), for [itself/himself/herself] and for its heirs, legal representatives, and assigns, and _____ (the "Covenantee").

1. In exchange for the Covenantor's covenant herein, the Covenantee _____ _____ _____ _____ _____.

2. In exchange for the consideration stated in paragraph 1 above, the receipt and sufficiency of which is hereby acknowledged by the Covenantor, the Covenantor covenants with the Covenantee never to institute any suit or action at law or in equity against the Covenantee by reason of any claim the Covenantor now has or may hereafter acquire related to: _____ _____.

This agreement was executed by the parties under seal on _____.

Covenantor: Covenantee:

_____   _____

_____   _____

This page intentionally blank.

RELEASE OF JUDGMENT

The Plaintiff, _____, hereby acknowledges that the judgment in this action has been fully satisfied by the Defendant, _____, and hereby releases and discharges said Defendant from any and all further liability for said judgment.

Dated: _____

_____

This page intentionally blank.

RELEASE OF LIENS

The undersigned [sub]contractor has furnished construction materials and/or labor in connection with repairs or construction at the property described as: (insert legal property description, street address, recording information, or other appropriate information)

(hereinafter called the "Premises"). The undersigned hereby releases all liens and rights to file liens against the Premises for any and all such materials or services provided through the date of this release.

The date of this release is _____.

Contractor/Subcontractor:

_____

_____

This page intentionally blank.

MECHANIC'S/MATERIALMAN'S LIEN WAIVER

The undersigned (the "Lienholder") has performed for and/or provided materials to the persons named below (the "Owner") at the address listed below under an agreement dated _____:

Services were performed for or materials were supplied to:

_____ (Name)

_____ (Address)

_____

_____

Materials were supplied and are located at the following address (if different from above):

_____

_____

_____

_____

The Lienholder performed the following services (if any) for the Owner:

The Lienholder, in consideration of payment for services and/or materials provided, hereby releases all property of the Owner and all improvements located on such property from any and all liens, rights, or claims, statutory or otherwise, that Lienholder may have by reason of providing services and/or materials related to the property and/or improvements related to the property.

The Lienholder hereby acknowledges that, as the Lienholder's voluntary act and deed, this Waiver releases the Lienholder's rights under the laws of the State of _____.

The date of this Waiver is _____.

_____ (Lienholder)

_____

_____

This page intentionally blank.

INDEMNIFICATION AGREEMENT

In exchange for _____ and other valuable consideration, the receipt and sufficiency of which is hereby acknowledged, the undersigned hereby agrees to indemnify and hold _____ _____ (the "Company") harmless from any claim, action, liability, or suit arising out of or in any way connected with the following:

In the event any claim reasonably believed by the Company to be subject to indemnification under this agreement is asserted against the Company, the Company will provide timely notice of such claim to the undersigned. The undersigned will thereafter, at its own expense, defend and protect the Company against such claim. Should the undersigned be unable or fail to so defend the Company, the Company shall have the right to defend or settle such claim, and the undersigned shall reimburse the Company for all settlements, judgments, fees, costs, expenses, and payments, including reasonable attorney's fees, incurred by the Company in connection with the discharge of such claim.

This agreement shall be governed by the laws of _____.

If any part of this agreement is adjudged invalid, illegal, or unenforceable, the remaining parts shall not be affected and shall remain in full force and effect.

This agreement shall be binding upon the parties, and upon their heirs, executors, personal representatives, administrators, and assigns. No person shall have a right or cause of action arising out of or resulting from this agreement except those who are parties to it and their successors in interest.

This instrument, including any attached exhibits and addenda, constitutes the entire agreement of the parties. No representations or promises have been made except those that are set out in this agreement. This agreement may not be modified except in writing signed by all the parties.

IN WITNESS WHEREOF the parties have signed this agreement under seal on _____.

_____   _____

_____   _____

This page intentionally blank.

AFFIDAVIT

The undersigned, being first duly sworn, deposes and says:

This affidavit was executed by me on _____.

_____

STATE OF   )
COUNTY OF   )

I certify that _____, who ❑ is personally known to me to be the person whose name is subscribed to the foregoing instrument ❑ produced _____ as identification, personally appeared before me on _____, and ❑ acknowledged the execution of the foregoing instrument ❑ acknowledged that (s)he is (Assistant) Secretary of _____ and that by authority duly given and as the act of the corporation, the foregoing instrument was signed in its name by its (Vice) President, sealed with its corporate seal, and attested by him/her as its (Assistant) Secretary.

_____
Notary Public, State of
My commission expires:

Index